FREE STUFF FOR HOME & GARDEN

The Free Stuff Editors

Director: Bruce Lansky
Editor: Tom Grady
Asst. Editors: Louise Delagran, Amy Rood

OUR PLEDGE

We have selected the best of all offers available. The suppliers have promised, in writing, to honor single-copy requests through 1981 – and beyond, as long as supplies last. We will monitor the suppliers and keep the book updated and accurate. We're dedicated to making this a book that really works.

Meadowbrook Press
18318 Minnetonka Blvd. • Deephaven, MN 55391

Design: Terry Dugan
Illustrations: Marcia Conley

Library of Congress Cataloging in Publication Data

Free stuff for home & garden

    Includes index.
    1. Free material.   I. Lansky, Bruce. II. Grady, Tom, 1951-
AG600.F68   011'.03   80-39692
ISBN 0-915658-27-5

First Printing February 1981

Printed in the United States of America
ISBN 0-915658-27-5
Copyright © 1981 by Bruce Lansky

Contents

About This Book

Like our previous directories of "free stuff" – for kids, cooks and parents – *Free Stuff for Home & Garden* is a collection of the best materials available to readers through the mail from hundreds of organizations around the country. This new book describes over 350 booklets, pamphlets, catalogs, newsletters and products that anyone who is buying or improving a home, renting an apartment, or tending a garden will find helpful. Covering everything from how to weatherproof your home to how to grow African violets, *Free Stuff for Home & Garden* is a comprehensive guide to information that will help you save money *and* add enjoyment to your life.

You can build this library of home and garden information for very little cost. Half of the items in the book are available for either a postcard or a self-addressed, stamped envelope. Because of the high cost of return postage, however, some of the organizations listed in the book require postage and handling costs that range from 10¢ to $1.00.

To put this book together we solicited materials from thousands of sources. Then we evaluated everything we received, selected what we thought were the best offers, and secured not only the supplier's permission to list a particular offer, but a written pledge that it will be available through 1981.

Though mistakes do happen, we've tried our best to make sure you get what you send for. And we would like to thank the companies, associations and agencies listed here for their interest and help in making this book possible.

Note on government publications: We've been in close contact with the government agencies whose publications are listed in *Free Stuff for Home & Garden*, and we have every assurance that these publications will be available through 1981. But because of the vagaries of government

Introduction

budgets and because of the volume of requests these agencies get, it's possible that some of their publications may be temporarily unavailable at certain times.

What's in This Book

1. Directions on how to send for
   - hundreds of booklets and pamphlets on buying, remodeling, restoring, decorating, insuring and cleaning your home;
   - plans and instructions for do-it-yourself projects like building decks, fences, storage sheds, room dividers and plant stands;
   - a wide range of materials on saving energy in the home, including information on insulating and weatherproofing, cutting your utility bills, heating with wood, and using solar and alternative forms of energy;
   - guides to planting and tending indoor and outdoor gardens, plus information on how to can and freeze your own produce;
   - catalogs of home plans, furniture, tools and seeds; and
   - sample copies of gardening magazines and newsletters.

2. Precise descriptions of the contents, format and length of each publication available. A **foldout** is a single sheet of paper folded up. A **booklet** is a small, staple-bound book; a **pamphlet** is a narrower booklet.

3. Excerpts and tips reprinted from some of the publications described, giving you a forecast of the kind of information contained in them. Also listed are examples of the kinds of products and publications available through the mail-order catalogs described in this book. These products and publications, called "Best Bets," can only be bought through the catalogs and **not** through *Free Stuff for Home & Garden*.

4. An index to direct you to all the materials on any particular topic.

How to Use This Book

Please follow all the directions as exactly as you can. The organizations that supply this "free stuff" are under no obligation to reply to requests that are improperly made.

- Please ask for only **one** copy of each item you're interested in.

- Make each request as brief as possible and always note what you've enclosed in your envelope. For instance, if you want to send for the very first item in the book, merely write:

  Please send me 1 copy of "What Every Home Buyer Should Know." I have enclosed 50¢.

  You may wish to photocopy and use the form provided on page 123.
- Always write your name and address on both the envelope and on the letter you send. Gummed, self-addressed labels are ideal.
- If the directions say to send a postcard (and many do), please comply with them. Suppliers can answer your requests more promptly if you do, and it saves you postage money. (Remember that the post office will not deliver a card that's smaller than 3-1/2 by 5-1/2 inches.)

- If the instructions say to send money, please enclose the fewest number of coins possible, and tape them to the letter you send so they won't rip or fall out of your envelope. (One piece of tape per coin is enough.) Please don't send stamps unless asked to.
- If the suppliers require a self-addressed, stamped envelope, it's very important that you fold up and enclose a **9"-long business envelope.** Most of the "free stuff" won't fit in a smaller envelope.
- Be prepared to wait 4 to 8 weeks for your materials to arrive. You could be surprised with a quicker reply, but you may also have to wait a little longer if a particular organization gets a lot of requests in a short period of time.

HOME

Buying & Renting

Basic Buying

A 12-page pamphlet on "What Every Home Buyer Should Know." Basic styles of homes are described and illustrated, with concise definitions of the important structural elements. Several pages are allowed for note-taking about particular homes.

Ask for: "What Every Home Buyer Should Know"
Send: 50¢
To: Housemaster of America
18 Hamilton St.
Bound Brook, NJ 08805

Home Buying

A 32-page booklet on "Wise Home Buying." The decision to buy and your readiness for the purchase of a home are discussed, followed by tips on finding the right house, inspecting it thoroughly, financing and purchasing. A glossary of terms related to home buying is included.

Ask for: "Wise Home Buying"
Send: a postcard
To: Consumer Information Ctr.
Dept. 598J
Pueblo, CO 81009

Home Buyer's Vocabulary

A 16-page booklet containing definitions of the essential terms that a home buyer should be familiar with. The terms are defined as they are commonly understood in the mortgage and real-estate industry. These definitions are intentionally general, nontechnical and brief.

Ask for: "Home Buyer's Vocabulary"
Send: a postcard
To: Consumer Information Ctr.
Dept. 601J
Pueblo, CO 81009

OLDER HOMES
Older homes deserve special attention in 9 areas before a prospective buyer signs on the dotted line. So check these items carefully: termite infestation and wood rot, structural failure, inadequate wiring, rundown heating plant, inadequate insulation, faulty plumbing, hot-water heater, roof and gutters, wet basements.

Real Estate

The 265-page Strout Realty catalog, which lists farm, ranch, recreational, commercial, motel, orchard and estate properties from all over the United States. Each property is described and priced; many are accompanied by photographs. Also includes a list of sales offices and details on Strout's national referral service.

Ask for: "Strout Realty Catalog"
Send: a postcard
To: Strout Realty
Plaza Towers – MP
Springfield, MO 65804

House Selection

An information-packed, 22-page booklet outlining the major considerations confronting the prospective homeowner. The booklet covers monthly payments, interest rates, sources of financing, housing types and locations, use of realtors, negotiating price, closing procedures and costs, and insurance.

Ask for: "The Househunter's Guide"
Send: a postcard
To: Househunter's Guide
Chicago Title Insurance Co.
Ste. 837
111 W. Washington St.
Chicago, IL 60602

MORTGAGES
- Is there a prepayment penalty clause?
- Is it an "open-end" mortgage that can accommodate future borrowing?
- What is the grace period for late payments?
- Do you have to pay "points" to get the mortgage?
- Does the lender require mortgage guarantee insurance?

Settlement

An informative, 40-page booklet on settlement costs in home buying. Among the topics considered are what happens and when; how to select an attorney, lender and settlement agent; and how to find out the home buyer's rights and obligations. Samples of the Uniform Settlement Statement form and worksheets are included.

Ask for: "Settlement Costs"
Send: $1.00
To: Consumer Information Ctr.
Dept. 160J
Pueblo, CO 81009

Settlement Costs
A HUD Guide
Revised Edition

Buying & Renting

HUD

The U.S. Department of Housing & Urban Development distributes many free publications to homeowners and renters. Information on renting vs. buying, mortgages, settlement, financing, insurance and other subjects is available to the public. Some of HUD's publications are listed on this page.

To receive any of this information, first check your phone book to see if there's an **Area** HUD office where you live. If there is, you can call or send a postcard to request the information you want.

If there is no Area office where you live, contact the nearest **Regional** HUD office (the addresses are listed on the following page) with your request.

(**Note:** when you make your request, ask for each publication you want by name and number. It's possible that each Area or Regional office may not have **all** the publications listed here, but they will do their best to provide the information you request.)

- "Your Housing Rights" HUD-401
- "Fact Sheet: Should You Rent or Buy a Home?" HUD-328-H (5)
- "Fact Sheet: HUD's Homeownership Subsidy Program" HUD-419-H (3)
- "Buying a Home? Don't Forget the Settlement Costs!" HUD-342-H (8)
- "Home Mortgage Insurance" HUD-43-F (8)
- "Having Problems Paying Your Mortgage?" HUD-426-PA (3)
- "Moving in ... with a Graduated Payment Mortgage" HUD H-317 (3)
- "Financing Condominium Housing" HUD-77-H (6)
- "HUD-FHA Comparison of Cooperative & Condominium Housing" HUD-321-F (5)
- "Let's Consider Cooperatives" HUD-17-H (8)
- "A Guide to Housing Rehabilitation Programs" HUD-NVACP-320 (4)
- "Mobile Home Financing Through HUD" HUD-401
- "Fact Sheet: Why Tenant Organizations?" HUD-339-H (3)

Region I

Public Information Officer
Regional Office of the Dept.
  of HUD
John F. Kennedy Federal
  Bldg.
Boston, MA 02203

Region II

Public Information Officer
Regional Office of the Dept.
  of HUD
26 Federal Plaza
New York, NY 10278

Region III

Public Information Officer
Regional Office of the Dept.
  of HUD
Curtis Bldg.
Sixth & Walnut Sts.
Philadelphia, PA 19106

Region IV

Public Information Officer
Regional Office of the Dept.
  of HUD
Richard B. Russell Federal
  Bldg.
75 Spring St. SW
Atlanta, GA 30303

Region V

Public Information Officer
Regional Office of the Dept.
  of HUD
300 S. Wacker Dr.
Chicago, IL 60606

Region VI

Public Information Officer
Regional Office of the Dept.
  of HUD
221 Lancaster Ave.
P.O. Box 2905
Ft. Worth, TX 76113

Region VII

Public Information Officer
Regional Office of the Dept.
  of HUD
Professional Bldg.
1103 Grand Ave.
Kansas City, MO 64106

Region VIII

Public Information Officer
Regional Office of the Dept.
  of HUD
Executive Tower
1405 Curtis St.
Denver, CO 80202

Region IX

Public Information Officer
Regional Office of the Dept.
  of HUD
450 Golden Gate Ave.
P.O. Box 36003
San Francisco, CA 94102

Region X

Public Information Officer
Regional Office of the Dept.
  of HUD
Arcade Plaza Bldg.
1321 Second Ave.
Seattle, WA 98101

Credit Laws

A comprehensive, 46-page booklet concerning credit-protection laws. The booklet addresses such issues as the cost of credit, applying for credit, credit histories and records, correcting credit mistakes and complaining about credit. A short glossary, index and lists of federal enforcement agencies and Federal Reserve banks are also included.

Ask for: "Consumer Handbook to Credit-Protection Laws"
Send: a postcard
To: Consumer Information Ctr.
    Dept. 606J
    Pueblo, CO 81009

Credit Guide

An informative, 36-page pamphlet on shopping for credit. The "finance charge" and "annual percentage rate" are defined, and suggestions about where to go for credit are offered. The pamphlet also provides useful tables for figuring specific payments based on annual percentage rates.

Ask for: "Credit Shopping Guide"
Send: $1.00
To: Consumer Information Ctr.
    Dept. 171J
    Pueblo, CO 81009

Appraisals

A 14-page pamphlet about real-estate appraisals. It explains what a real-estate appraisal is, what it will tell you, why and when you should have an appraisal made and how to find a qualified professional appraiser. The pamphlet also explains the 3 professional designations awarded by the Society of Real Estate Appraisers.

Ask for: "What Is an Appraisal?"
Send: a 9" self-addressed, stamped envelope
To: Robert E. Palmer
    Soc. of Real Estate Appraisers
    Dept. PR
    645 N. Michigan Ave.
    Chicago, IL 60611

PURPOSE

There are many good reasons for having an appraisal made of your property. Among them are

- to obtain a professional opinion of the present value of a home or property you may wish to buy or sell.
- to verify damage claims resulting from fire, rain, hail, windstorms and other disasters.

Reprinted with permission of the Society of Real Estate Appraisers.

Appraisals

A pamphlet presenting questions and answers about the appraisal profession. Consumer tips on selecting an appraiser are included. The pamphlet also supplies a description of the requirements behind the professional designations of members of the American Society of Appraisers.

Ask for: "Information on the Appraisal Profession"
Send: a 9″ self-addressed, stamped envelope
To: American Society of Appraisers
Dept. C
Dulles International Airport
P.O. Box 17265
Washington, DC 20041

APPRAISERS
Don't hesitate to ask for credentials. This includes the appraiser's educational background, experience with your type of property and certification by written examination. Also, how recently an appraiser either passed such an examination or completed relevant continuing education should be considered.

Condo Q & A

A 52-page, illustrated booklet answering the basic questions most people have about condominiums. Sample topics include a definition of a condo, points to consider when buying one, rental conversions, the basic documents of condominium ownership and the National Housing Act. A glossary is also provided.

Ask for: "Questions about Condominiums"
Send: a postcard
To: Consumer Information Ctr.
Dept. 594J
Pueblo, CO 81009

Questions About Condominiums
What to ask before you buy

Buying Condos

A foldout for anyone interested in buying a condominium. It provides a checklist of questions to ask, questions that are often different from those asked by renters or single-family home buyers. It also covers such topics as the construction of the building, personal requirements, and the rules, insurance, budget and policy concerning absentee owners and management.

Ask for: "Consumer's Guide to Buying a Residential Condominium"
Send: a postcard
To: Inst. of Real Estate Management
Consumer Information Dept.
430 N. Michigan Ave.
Chicago, IL 60611

BUDGET
Is a proposed budget for the operation of the building provided? Who prepared the budget? Are the maintenance fees sufficient? This is especially important in a conversion. In an established condominium association, the purchaser should ask to see a copy of the financial statement. A review of the statement would also reveal the amount the association has in reserves.

Buying & Renting

Renting

An informative, 40-page booklet on "Wise Rental Practices." Some of the topics discussed are how to determine what rent you can afford, where to look for an apartment, how to learn your fair housing rights, how to distinguish between unlawful and lawful rules and regulations, and how to define the responsibilities of renters and landlords. A list of HUD field-office jurisdictions is included.

Ask for: "Wise Rental Practices"
Send: a postcard
To: Consumer Information Ctr.
Dept. 599J
Pueblo, CO 81009

Wise Rental Practices

Tenants

A foldout for home and apartment renters published by the Insurance Information Institute. The foldout explains what tenant's insurance is, what normal tenant policies cover (such as personal belongings, liability to others and additional living expenses for emergencies), how to determine your insurance needs and how to shop for tenant's insurance.

Ask for: "Tenant's Insurance Basics"
Send: a postcard
To: Insurance Information Inst.
110 William St.–FS
New York, NY 10038

SOME FACTS

As a tenant, you probably own furniture, appliances, a wardrobe and other valuable items. Some tenants assume that their personal belongings are insured against loss or damage by the landlord's policy. That is not true. Your landlord probably has insurance to cover the house or apartment building, but it does not include coverage for your personal belongings.

Insurance

A 24-page booklet about insurance that provides a brief overview of the kinds of insurance available to homeowners, condominium and mobile-home owners, and renters. Property and liability insurance (and their respective costs) are discussed in some detail.

Ask for: "A Family Guide to Auto & Home Insurance"
Send: a postcard
To: Insurance Information Inst.
110 William St. – FS
New York, NY 10038

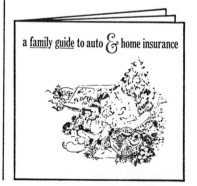

a family guide to auto & home insurance

Building & Remodeling

Building Terms

A 16-page booklet that consists of a homeowner's glossary of basic building terms. From acoustical tile to weep hole, this publication defines terms used in home construction, repair and maintenance. While not comprehensive, it does provide a quick reference for homeowners unfamiliar with building terminology.

Ask for: "Homeowner's Glossary of Building Terms"
Send: a postcard
To: Consumer Information Ctr.
Dept. 593J
Pueblo, CO 81009

DEFINITIONS
- Bearing wall: a wall that supports a floor or roof of a building.
- Cornice: a horizontal projection at the top of a wall or under the overhanging part of the roof.
- Lally column: a steel tube (sometimes filled with concrete) that is used to support girders or other floor beams.

House Basics

A 32-page booklet on "House Building Basics." Beginning with a glossary, this guide to "getting to know your house" offers 14 sections on the construction of modern frame houses. From laying the foundation through flooring, walls, siding, ceilings and roofs, here is all the necessary information for those interested in building their own homes from the ground up.

Ask for: "House Building Basics"
Send: $1.00
To: American Plywood Assn.
Office Services Dept.
P.O. Box 11700
Tacoma, WA 98411

THE FOUNDATION
Laying out a foundation is the critical beginning in house construction. It is a simple but extremely important process and requires careful work. If you make sure the foundation is **square** and **level**, you will find all later jobs – from rough carpentry through finished construction and installation of cabinetry – are made much easier.

Home Plans

Three home plan catalogs, available separately, that describe and illustrate a variety of pre-designed traditional and contemporary homes that you can build yourself – using blueprints that can be ordered. Each catalog presents sketches of dozens of homes plus interior floor plans, including dimensions.

- **"New Home Trends"**
- **"Family Room Homes"**
- **"Hillside Home Plans"**

Ask for: each catalog that you want by name
Send: $1.00 for **each**
To: Home Building Plan Service, Inc.
    2235 N.E. Sandy Blvd., Studio FS
    Portland, OR 97232

Home Plans

Four catalogs, available separately, that present floor plans and pictures of finished homes you can build yourself – with blueprints you can order from the catalogs.

- **"Traditional 1-Story Homes"**
- **"Modern/Contemporary 1-Story Homes"**
- **"1½-and 2-Story Homes" (Vol. 1)**
- **"1½ and 2-Story Homes" (Vol. 2)**

(Volumes 1 & 2 do not duplicate one another; they can be ordered separately.)

Ask for: each catalog you want by name
Send: $1.00 for **each**
To: Sam Benedict
    Dept. MP
    20 Marietta St. NW, Ste. 1617
    Atlanta, GA 30303

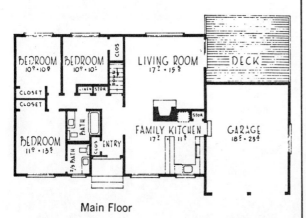

Main Floor

Building & Remodeling

Down Under

A 6-page information packet on underground housing. Basic information on the benefits of underground living is provided, and one style of underground home is described. Details about the new *Underground House Book* are also included.

Ask for: "Underground House Plans"
Send: a postcard
To: Garden Way Publishing
Dept. A563
Charlotte, VT 05445

Second Homes

A 22-page booklet describing plans available for a variety of second homes. Each plan includes a color illustration of the completed home, detailed floor plans and individual highlights. An order form with instructions is provided.

Ask for: "The Second Home"
Send: $1.00
To: Home Building Plan Service, Inc.
2235 N.E. Sandy Blvd., Studio FS
Portland, OR 97232

Vacation Homes

A 16-page booklet showing vacation homes designed with red cedar shingles and shakes. The booklet contains color photographs of beach cabins, leisure homes, mountain retreats and hill-top hideaways, both in exterior and interior shots. Also included are names of architects whose houses are pictured and 4 addresses to which the reader can write for plans of finished houses.

Ask for: "Vacation Homes"
Send: 35¢
To: Red Cedar Shingle & Handsplit
Shake Bureau
515 116th Ave. NE, Ste. 275
Bellevue, WA 98004

Q & A
How much earth goes on the roof? 18 to 36 inches seems best. More depth taxes the bearing capacity of the roof too much – soil weighs 100-200 pounds/cubic foot, more when wet. Too little soil limits roof vegetation. It also spells diminishing returns in heat retention.

THE SECOND HOME

Western Wood does it like nothing else can.

Leaking Roofs

A foldout providing useful information on how to inspect your roof for leaks. The foldout also shows how to identify problem areas before they develop into leaks, thus enabling you to prevent expensive repairs to other parts of the house.

Ask for: "Homeowner's Guide for Roof Inspection"
Send: a postcard
To: Ken Schweikhart, Adv. Mgr.
Celotex Corp.
1500 N. Dale Mabry Hwy.
Tampa, FL 33607

Roofing

A 16-page pamphlet to aid homeowners in selecting quality roofing. Among the topics considered are roof replacement, available coverings, fire and wind resistance, color, do-it-yourself techniques and the process of selecting a roofer.

Ask for: "Homeowner's Guide to Quality Roofing"
Send: 35¢
To: Asphalt Roofing Mfrs. Assn.
℅ SR&A
355 Lexington Ave.
New York, NY 10017

Cedar Roofs

A color foldout for people thinking about replacing their roofs. The foldout explains how you can avoid a mess and gain a better insulated roof by putting a new cedar shingle or shake roof over your old roof. Detailed "how-to" information and data on tools and techniques are provided. Several before and after pictures of "over-roofed" houses are also included.

Ask for: "Over-Roof with Cedar"
Send: 10¢
To: Red Cedar Shingle & Handsplit
Shake Bureau
515 116th Ave. NE, Ste. 275
Bellevue, WA 98004

MAINTENANCE
Keep gutters, downspouts and roof surfaces clear of leaves, twigs and litter. Keep trees trimmed to prevent scraping. Don't walk on roofing – it's dangerous and can damage the shingles. When removing snow or ice, be careful not to damage the roof with whatever tools are used.

Building & Remodeling

Cedar

A color foldout about economy-grade red cedar shingles and shakes. It explains that knots and imperfections make these shingles and shakes unsuitable for use on roofs and most exterior walls, but their beauty and low cost make them desirable for other uses. The foldout presents 13 ways to use the economy grade.

Ask for: "How to Do It...and Save"
Send: 10¢
To: Red Cedar Shingle & Handsplit
Shake Bureau
515 116th Ave. NE, Ste. 275
Bellevue, WA 98004

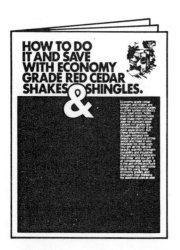

Home Siding

A 15-page booklet on choosing and installing siding for your house. The booklet discusses the benefits of siding in general and considers the advantages of the different kinds of siding on the market. Also answers questions you may have on cost, financing and maintenance of siding.

Ask for: "A Homeowner's Guide to Choosing Siding"
Send: a postcard
To: Aluminum Siding Information
Bureau
250 West 57th St.
New York, NY 10019

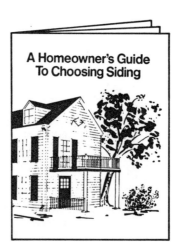

Windows & Doors

Two pamphlets with answers to your questions about windows and doors. Common questions related to planning, care, beauty, brands, energy and installation are answered, and various types of windows are described.

Ask for: "The Window and Gliding Door Answer Book" and "Easy Window and Gliding Door Installation"
Send: a postcard
To: Andersen Corp.
Dept. WD & L-9
Bayport, MN 55003

Q & A
What about winter heat loss? A window made of wood and using double-pane insulating glass can reduce heat loss through the window area by at least 47% (That's compared to a single-pane window without storms.) Weathertight windows and gliding doors can, in effect, "create" winter heat by bringing sunlight into your home and trapping its warmth.

Moisture

A 14-page pamphlet for anyone with damp masonry walls (brick, concrete, concrete block, cinder block or stucco). The pamphlet helps diagnose the cause of the moisture and presents a line of products to correct the problem. It explains how to prepare masonry surfaces and apply sealers to prevent moisture from penetrating.

Ask for: "How to Waterproof Masonry Walls"
Send: 25¢
To: How to Waterproof Masonry Walls
United Gilsonite Labs.
Dept. 961
Scranton, PA 18501

Waterproofing

A 19-page pamphlet offering instruction on do-it-yourself basement waterproofing with epoxy. Deals with problems encountered on various types of building sites, roof water leaks, subsurface drainage, construction modes that make for better seals, condensation, dehumidification and sump pumps.

Ask for: "Waterproofing"
Send: a 9″ self-addressed, stamped envelope
To: Dur-A-Flex, Inc.
Dept. FSFH
P.O. Box 14490
Hartford, CT 06114

WATER DROPS
Are those drops of water coming in through the concrete or condensing from the air? To find out, tape a piece of metal or glass to the surface. After a few days, check both sides of it. If the room side is dry and the wall is wet, you know that all the water is coming through the wall. Conversely, if the wall side is dry and the room side is wet, all the water is from the air.

Waterproofing Material

A sample of "Flashband," a peel-and-stick, aluminum-faced, instant sealing and waterproofing strip. This do-it-yourself roll aluminum is easily applied without any special tools and can be painted over.

Ask for: "Flashband"
Send: a 9″ self-addressed, stamped envelope
To: 3E Corp.
Dept. MP1
P.O. Box 177
Somerdale, NJ 08083

Building & Remodeling

Moisture Damage

An informative, full-color foldout on preventing moisture damage. This material explains how moisture damages a home's interior and exterior paint and its structural materials as a result of insufficient ventilation. Specific methods for protecting homes from moisture damage are offered.

Ask for: "Preventing Moisture Damage"
Send: 25¢ and a 9″ self-addressed, stamped envelope
To: Consumer Pamphlets
  % NPCA
  1500 Rhode Island Ave. NW
  Washington, DC 20005

PROTECTION
- To keep vapor from condensing on cold surfaces, ventilate attic well.
- When bathing, allow moisture to escape through door or window.
- Install exhaust fan in kitchen to keep excess humidity from damaging your home.

Storm Damage

A full-color foldout on the best methods for repairing home damage caused by winter storms. Ice dams and their results are explained in detail. The foldout also supplies helpful information about preventive measures and repair methods.

Ask for: "RX for Winter Storm-Damaged Homes"
Send: 25¢ and a 9″ self-addressed, stamped envelope
To: Consumer Pamphlets
  % NPCA
  1500 Rhode Island Ave. NW
  Washington, DC 20005

ICE DAMS
Many types of damage can result from roof ice-dam formation, such as
- structural damage to roofs, porches and walls
- rotting of wood structural members from soaked insulation
- crumbling of plaster ceilings and walls

Wood Decay

An 18-page booklet on the prevention and control of wood decay in houses. General safeguards are recommended, followed by specific precautions for woodwork that is close to the ground and parts of houses that are commonly exposed to rain. Helpful illustrations demonstrate both good and poor practices.

Ask for: "Wood Decay in Houses" (G73)
Send: a postcard
To: Publications Div.
  Office of Governmental and Public Affairs
  U.S. Dept. of Agriculture
  Washington, DC 20250

Wood Decay in Houses
How to Prevent and Control It

Wood Products

A booklet that discusses some of the properties of wood including its strength, durability and insulating qualities. Also a foldout listing many publications available from the American Wood Council. This list includes booklets on design and decorating ideas, as well as practical guides to construction with wood.

Ask for: "Some Little Known Facts About Wood" and/or "A Reader's Guide to Wood Products"
Send: a postcard
To: Elizabeth Hord
American Wood Council
1619 Massachusetts Ave. NW
Washington, DC 20036

PROPERTIES
The strength of wood surprises most people. For example, a wood block just 1" square and 2-1/4" long can support 5 tons on its end. In fact, pound for pound, wood can be stronger than steel. This great strength comes from the natural strength of wood's cells. And the lignin that cements the cells together is not only strong; it's elastic.

Remodeling

A 20-page booklet on "Easy Changes, Large and Small." Plans for extensions, additions and room conversions are included, as are some suggestions for outdoor remodeling to give your home a new look. Storage closets, nooks and walls are described with specific building hints.

Ask for: "Easy Changes, Large and Small"
Send: $1.00
To: American Plywood Assn.
Office Services Dept.
P.O. Box 11700
Tacoma, WA 98411

Easy changes, large and small.

Improvements

An informative foldout outlining considerations faced by families planning home improvements. Covers research, planning, contractor selection and negotiation. A major portion of the foldout is about household surfaces – how to select them on the basis of hardness, surface thickness and ease of maintenance.

Ask for: "Doing It Over and Maintaining Your Investment"
Send: a postcard
To: The Clorox Co.
Consumer Services Dept.
P.O. Box 24305FS
Oakland, CA 94623

Doing It Over and Maintaining Your Investment

Block Cement

Four publications about building cement block structures with Surewall Surface Bonding Cement instead of conventional mortar. They provide detailed information on using cement and plans for several structures, including a garage, picnic table, barbecue grill, utility shed and more.

- **"Building with Surewall Manual"**
- **"Surewall Project Pamphlet"**
- **"Surewall Table Plans"**
- **"Surewall Garage Plans"**

Ask for: each publication you want by name
Send: a postcard
To: Robert E. Post, Sr.
The Inca Co.
Stanton & Empire St.
Wilkes-Barre, PA 18702

Concrete

Two pages of questions and answers concerning concrete. The 8 most-asked questions, dealing with ordering, mixing, pouring, curing, scaling and temperature, are answered. Illustrations demonstrate how to make a false "expansion joint" and how to create a simulated flagstone look.

Ask for: "Hard Answers to Concrete Questions" (X194A)
Send: 75¢
To: Popular Mechanics
Dept. MP
P.O. Box 1014, Radio City Sta.
New York, NY 10101

CURING
This means keeping fresh concrete damp so that the moisture doesn't evaporate too rapidly during hydration. To cure, cover the freshly poured surface with material such as burlap. Then, depending on temperature and humidity, use a garden hose to moisten burlap once or twice daily. Keep concrete covered and moist 5-7 days.

Brick Steps

Two pages of instructions on building brick and masonry steps. Planning, estimating and foundations are considered, as are bonds, mortar and joints. This information is followed by material on the subject of formwork, pouring and finishing for concrete steps. Illustrations are included.

Ask for: "How to Build Brick and Masonry Steps"
Send: 75¢
To: Popular Mechanics
Dept. MP
P.O. Box 1014, Radio City Sta.
New York, NY 10101

Troweling

An illustrated, 24-page pamphlet of "Troweling Tips and Techniques" for the home craftsperson. This basic guide includes information on the tools necessary for working with a variety of materials including concrete, concrete blocks, bricks and wallboard, as well as general instructions for projects using these materials.

Ask for: "Troweling Tips and Techniques"
Send: 75¢
To: G. W. Miller
Marshalltown Trowel Co.
P.O. Box 738
Marshalltown, IA 50158

Tools

An 88-page catalog of tools for both professionals and amateurs. Plastering, carpentry and masonry equipment are included, as are such accessories as tool bags and pouches. Heavy duty professional machinery is also available.

Ask for: "Goldblatt Tool Catalog"
Send: a postcard
To: Goldblatt Tool Co.
585 Osage
Kansas City, KS 66110

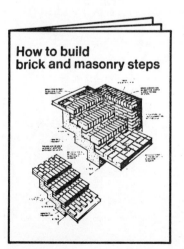

How to build brick and masonry steps

CONCRETE WALL
A number of ways exist to finish your concrete wall. Masonry paint is perfectly suited for use on such walls, and waterproof varieties are available, if required. To use paneling, dry wall, or any other inside wall material, first nail furring strips to the wall using masonry nails; then fasten your wall material to the furring strips.

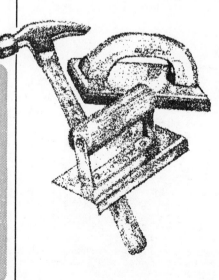

Building & Remodeling

Outdoor Plans

A 16-page booklet of plans for outdoor projects made with pressure-treated, preserved, all-weather wood. Plans for a patio, a garden bench, fences and a greenhouse are among those included. A sample bill of materials and illustrated instructions for each project are provided.

Ask for: "Great Plans for Great Outdoor Projects"
Send: 50¢
To: W. Page
Osmose FS1
980 Ellicott St.
Buffalo, NY 14209

Decks

An 8-page idea booklet for construction of wood decks and screens for swimming pools. Has photos of finished decks, as well as plans and specifications for building. Offers options beyond the traditional wrap-around, doughnut-shaped deck. Decks provide a cooler, fast-drying surface for playing or entertaining. Also pictures an idea for a wood gazebo.

Ask for: "Decks for Pools"
Send: 35¢
To: Western Wood Products Assn.
Dept. P-14
Yeon Bldg.
Portlar.d, OR 97204

BEFORE CUTTING
Before cutting your material, be certain you review all steps of construction and verify all dimensions. Make sure your planned structure conforms to all local building codes. Consider pool height, land contours and existing plantings when setting elevations for the pool deck and lower deck, as well as the fence wall that separates the two.

Deck Plans

An 8-page, illustrated booklet on "Redwood Deck Construction." The physical advantages of redwood are discussed, with specific information about redwood grades, patterns and construction plans. Tips for special situations, such as slopes, rooftops and decking over concrete, are also mentioned.

Ask for: "Redwood Deck Construction" (3C2-5)
Send: 30¢
To: Redwood Deck Construction
Dept. STUFF
California Redwood Assn.
One Lombard St.
San Francisco, CA 94111

Garden Storage

A 16-page booklet for the home craftsperson who wants to build a number of different storage sheds – one for garden tools, one for firewood, one for bicycles and barbecues. Black-and-white photographs of each of the projects plus building plans are provided.

Ask for: "Garden Living & Storage" (FS-15)
Send: 50¢
To: Western Wood Products Assn.
Dept. FS-15
1500 Yeon Bldg.
Portland, OR 97204

Redwood Garden

A 12-page, illustrated booklet of plans for a variety of redwood garden structures including fences, dividers, decks and benches. Information on buying redwood, choosing the proper grades for various uses, and selecting finishes is also included.

Ask for: "Garden Structures You Can Build" (3C9)
Send: 40¢
To: Garden Structures You Can Build
Dept. STUFF
California Redwood Assn.
One Lombard St.
San Francisco, CA 94111

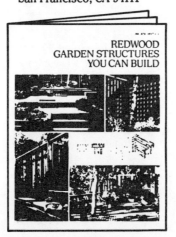

Redwood Fences

A 12-page, full-color booklet and an illustrated data sheet on redwood fences. The booklet describes the advantages of redwood fencing and illustrates a number of traditional and innovative designs. The data sheet provides the details of the actual construction.

Ask for: "Redwood Fences" and "Building a Redwood Fence" (3C2-3)
Send: 60¢
To: Redwood Fences
Dept. STUFF
California Redwood Assn.
One Lombard St.
San Francisco, CA 94111

FENCE DESIGNS
One of the first things in designing a fence is to decide how you want it to function. Keep in mind that there probably is no such thing as a purely decorative fence. A fence will always function in some way – by controlling or admitting sunlight, or by acting as either a physical or a visual barrier.

Building & Remodeling

Signs & Vanes

Two foldouts about old-fashioned copper weathervanes and hand-lettered, personalized copper shingles. The foldouts include pictures and descriptions of available styles, prices and order blanks. They briefly explain the processes used to make and finish the copper signs and vanes.

Ask for: "Copper Shingles" and "Weathervanes"
Send: a 15¢ stamp
To: Ship 'n Out Inc.
681 Harmony Rd.
Pawling, NY 12564

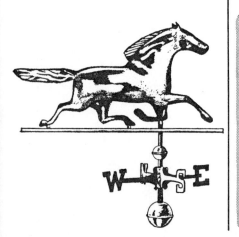

Useful Books

A comprehensive, 66-page catalog of books on many subjects of interest to the homeowner. Sample topics include remodeling, do-it-yourself projects, carpentry and building. Instructions for ordering are included.

Ask for: "Mother's Bookshelf Catalog"
Send: a postcard
To: Mother's Bookshelf
Dept. FS
P.O. Box 70
Hendersonville, NC 28791

BEST BETS
- *The Encyclopedia of Wood* (Forest Products Laboratory)
- *The Practical Carpenter* (Andrew Perry)
- *How to Inspect a House* (George Hoffman)
- *The Little House* (Leslie Armstrong)

Government Catalogs

Two catalogs from the U.S. Government Printing Office that list dozens of government publications on home construction, home maintenance and homeowning that can be purchased through the mail.

Ask for: "The Home" (SB-041) and "Housing, Urban and Rural Development" (SB-280)
Send: a postcard
To: Superintendent of Documents
U.S. Government Printing Office
Washington, DC 20402

BEST BETS
- "House Construction: How to Reduce Costs." A booklet that summarizes a wide variety of information on choosing the location and design of your new house.
- "Home Buyer's Estimator of Monthly Housing Cost." A guide to help you determine whether you can afford the home you choose.

Painting & Finishing

Painting & Finishing

Painting Tips

A 26-page booklet on exterior and interior painting. Such topics as surface preparation, paint selection, application, whitewashing and paint failures are considered. Charts to aid in paint selection and illustrations of specific tasks are also included.

Ask for: "Painting Inside and Out" (G222)
Send: a postcard
To: Publications Div.
Office of Governmental and Public Affairs
U.S. Dept. of Agriculture
Washington, DC 20250

Exteriors

A full-color foldout on the subject of painting exteriors. Some of the information presented includes how to carry out a typical exterior paint project from beginning to end; some common paint problems and how to prevent them; what types of coatings to use in particular areas; and suggested color schemes.

Ask for: "Painting Exteriors"
Send: 25¢ and a 9″ self-addressed, stamped envelope
To: Consumer Pamphlets
% NPCA
1500 Rhode Island Ave. NW
Washington, DC 20005

Latex Paints

A full-color foldout concerning the proper use of latex paints. This primer on interior and exterior latex paints explains what they are, what they can do and how to use them most effectively. Helpful for the beginning painter.

Ask for: "Using Latex Paints"
Send: 25¢ and a 9″ self-addressed, stamped envelope
To: Consumer Pamphlets
% NPCA
1500 Rhode Island Ave. NW
Washington, DC 20005

PAINT SAFETY
Never paint in a completely closed room, nor in a room where there is an open flame or fire. Some fumes can be especially harmful to infants, children, canaries and other delicate pets. Use a sturdy stepladder or other support when painting high places. Avoid any electrical wiring within the area of work.

APPEARANCE
Good quality latex paints give clean, bright colors and offer excellent durability. An exterior surface coated with latex paint may show the dirt sooner, but the appearance can be readily restored by washing with mild detergent and water.

Paint Colors

A full-color foldout intended to aid the consumer in choosing the best paint colors. Among the topics considered are the uses of color; special paint styling tricks with color; color do's and don'ts; and helpful tips for selecting paint colors from chips.

Ask for: "Choosing Paint Colors"
Send: 25¢ and a 9″ self-addressed, stamped envelope
To: Consumer Pamphlets
%NPCA
1500 Rhode Island Ave. NW
Washington, DC 20005

Milk Paint

A foldout about genuine, old-fashioned, homemade milk paint. Milk paint can be used to authentically restore period furniture, early houses, stenciled walls, weathered signs, floors and cupboards, walls and woodwork. Description, instructions, and answers to frequently asked questions are included, along with an order form and color samples.

Ask for: "Old-Fashioned Milk Paint"
Send: 60¢ (in stamps or coin)
To: Old Fashioned Milk Paint Co.
North Main
Groton, MA 01450

Interiors

A full-color foldout on painting interiors. The information includes details on how to carry out a typical interior paint project from beginning to end. The foldout also suggests color do's and don'ts and what type of paint to use in various areas of the home.

Ask for: "Painting Interiors"
Send: 25¢ and a 9″ self-addressed, stamped envelope
To: Consumer Pamphlets
%NPCA
1500 Rhode Island Ave. NW
Washington, DC 20005

LIGHT COLORS
- Reflect more light
- Seem lighter in weight
- Make objects seem larger
- Make objects seem farther away
- Make you feel cheerful

PAINTING CEILINGS
When painting a ceiling, work across the width – rather than the length – of the room. This enables you to begin a second lap before the first has completely dried. Never try to paint a strip more than 2′ wide both for lapping and for safety purposes.

Painting & Finishing

Wood Finishing

A 16-page pamphlet for beginners who want to finish or refinish wood. The pamphlet explains how to remove old paint, shellac or other finishes, how to prepare bare wood for finishing and how to select and apply new stain and protective finishes. It also points out which old finishes need to be completely removed and which don't. Includes a color chart of natural wood and color stains.

Ask for: "The Finishing Touch"
Send: 25¢
To: The Finishing Touch
United Gilsonite Labs.
Dept. 960
Scranton, PA 18501

TIPS
- Sand with the grain only. Cross-grain sanding will produce scratches that will show through the finish.
- Work at eye level. It's the only way to judge results.
- Good lighting is a must.
- Do the hard parts – table bottoms, chair legs and similar areas – first.

Wood Finishing

A 16-page pamphlet of wood finishing tips. Information is included on the selection and sanding of new wood and the evaluation of soundness, stripping and sanding of old wood. The pamphlet also discusses paneling, flooring, antiques and finishing materials.

Ask for: "Tips on Woodfinishing"
Send: a postcard
To: Minwax Co., Inc.
Dept. FS
P.O. Box 995
Clifton, NJ 07014

Refinishing

A 25-page booklet about stripping and refinishing all kinds of surfaces: exterior and interior walls, trim, baseboards, doors, cabinets, furniture, wood floors, wallpaper and boats. It presents a line of refinishing products and many tips on doing this kind of work. Also includes a section on cleaning paint brushes, even old, hard-caked ones.

Ask for: "Latest and Best Methods in Refinishing: A Complete Guide"
Send: 50¢
To: Wilson Imperial Co.
117 Chestnut St.
Newark, NJ 07105

FURNITURE TIPS
- A piece of steel wool on a lollipop stick makes it easy to remove finish from carvings.
- Use steel wool entwined in a string for removing finish from spindles.
- Use fine steel brush for mouldings.
- Patch small holes with stick shellac or wood putty.

Wood Furniture

A full-color foldout on the entire process of refinishing wood furniture. This guide to refinishing previously finished and unfinished furniture from beginning to end explains the details of stripping, sanding, bleaching, staining, filling and finishing.

Ask for: "Refinishing Wood Furniture"
Send: 25¢ and a 9" self-addressed, stamped envelope
To: Consumer Pamphlets
% NPCA
1500 Rhode Island Ave. NW
Washington, DC 20005

Floor Refinishing

An 8-page booklet on finishing or refinishing hardwood flooring. This manual offers detailed, illustrated instructions for each step, including preparation, sanding and finishing. Various types of finish are described, and a note on protecting the finish is included.

Ask for: "Hardwood Flooring Finishing/Refinishing Manual"
Send: 50¢
To: Mr. H. F. Fingerman
Oak Flooring Inst.
804 Sterick Bldg.
Memphis, TN 38103

Wood Staining

A 22-page pamphlet on staining wood in the home. Tells how to select stains and apply them properly. Gives information on wood preparation, shading and toning, wood protection, reduction of grain contrast, color selection and mixing, new vs. previously finished wood, touch-ups and spray staining.

Ask for: "Simple Systems for Wood Staining and Finishing"
Send: a 9" self-addressed, stamped envelope
To: Deft, Inc.
Dept. MPF
17451 Von Karman Ave.
Irvine, CA 92714

SURFACE PREPARATION

To completely refinish an old piece of wood furniture, it is often necessary to remove all of the old finish before staining or other wood-finishing operations can be properly carried out. Use a good grade of commercially prepared chemical paint and varnish remover. The nonflammable, wax-free varieties are safest and easiest to use.

SPRAY STAINING

Be sure wood is clean, sanded and dust-free. Cover adjacent areas where over-spray may settle. Use in a warm, well-ventilated area. Shake can according to label instructions. Spray with rapid, uniform strokes, holding can 10-12" from surface. Overlap strokes to assure an even coat. To deepen color, apply additional coats. Do not sand prior to applying wood finish.

Saving Energy

Saving Energy

Energy Savers

A 4-page checklist to aid consumers in determining their energy use. A variety of questions in several areas offers readers an opportunity to make themselves more aware of ways in which they may be wasting energy. The answers to these questions emphasize money-savings tips.

Ask for: "Save Your Dollar Leaks: Save Energy" (Pub. 887)
Send: a postcard
To: Ms. Nancy B. Sweet, Pub. Editor
    P.O. Box 5404MSU
    Mississippi Coop. Extension
      Service
    Mississippi State, MS 39762

Energy Leaks

An 8-page booklet about ways to save energy in the home. It tells how to find and seal leaks around windows, doors, cracks, holes, electrical outlets and other places. It briefly discusses wall and attic insulation and explains how to save money by insulating your water heater.

Ask for: "The Home Energy-Savings Book #22"
Send: a postcard
To: Shell Oil Co.
    P.O. Box 61609
    Houston, TX 77208

TIPS
- Foundation seal: Check for cracks along the outside wall between the concrete foundation and house. Stuff with oakum caulking rope and caulk over it.
- Fireplace: Close damper tightly when not in use. If there is no damper, cover the opening with wood. Caulk cracks where fireplace meets wall.

Saving

A short foldout describing ways to cut home heating and cooling bills. Includes tips on insulation, windows, doors, air flow, thermostats, humidity, and equipment selection and maintenance. Also listed are ways to save energy by planning the use and placement of major appliances.

Ask for: "22 Ways to Save Energy"
Send: a 9" self-addressed, stamped envelope
To: BDP Co.
    Advertising Dept. MP
    7310 W. Morris St.
    Indianapolis, IN 46231

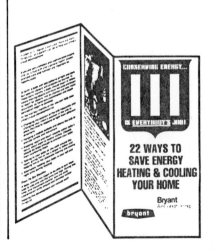

Energy Tips

Four publications from the Department of Energy about energy and energy-related topics. One presents hundreds of tips on how to save energy; one suggests what energy considerations you should take into account when buying or building a home; one explains how to get information about solar energy; another lists other DOE publications you can send for.

- **"Tips for Energy Savers"** (EDM-064, English)
- **"Energy-Saving Checklist for Home Builders, Buyers and Owners"** (EDM-344)
- **"Where to Find Information about Solar Energy"** (EDM-818)
- **"Selected Department of Energy Publications"** bibliography

Ask for: each pamphlet you want by name and number
Send: a postcard
To: Energy
P.O. Box 62
Oak Ridge, TN 37830

SAVING ENERGY

- Lower your thermostat to 65°F. during the day and 55°F. at night.
- Keep windows near your thermostat tightly closed.
- Clean or replace the filter in your forced-air heating system each month.
- Dust or vacuum radiator surfaces frequently. Dust and grime impede the flow of heat. And if the radiators need painting, use flat paint, preferably black. It radiates heat better than glossy.
- Keep draperies and shades open in sunny windows; close them at night.

From "Tips for Energy Savers"

Energy Savings

Four booklets that present ways to save energy (particularly natural gas) by insulating, weatherproofing and ventilating your home; by maintaining equipment properly; by choosing the right glass for your windows or modifying the present ones; and by picking energy-efficient appliances.

Ask for: "ESP Energy Savings Payback," "The Energy Savings Book," "How to Conserve Energy at Home" and/or "The Future Belongs to the Efficient"
Send: a postcard
To: Entex, Inc.
Sales Dept.
P.O. Box 2628
Houston, TX 77001

REFRIGERATOR TIPS

- Keep it full – but without overcrowding. A half-empty appliance uses more energy, because air is harder to keep cold than chilled foods and liquids.
- When going away, reset temperature controls on refrigerator and freezer to a lower number (less cooling). Since door will remain closed, food will keep cool.

Utility Bills

A 12-page pamphlet designed to help you understand your utility bill. Useful definitions, instructions on meter reading, suggestions for applying your meter-reading skills and a breakdown of all the codes on utility bills are provided. Also included is a chart that illustrates the average annual energy consumption and cost estimates for major appliances.

Ask for: "How to Understand Your Utility Bill"
Send: a postcard
To: Consumer Information Ctr.
Dept. 602J
Pueblo, CO 81009

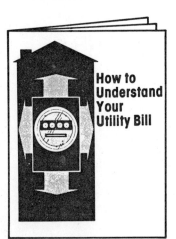

How to Understand Your Utility Bill

Natural Gas

A 12-page pamphlet that explains the natural gas shortage and rise in price. The pamphlet reassures home users that they have priority over commercial and industrial users and that more gas will be found as competitive prices make it worth looking for. It also contains some conservation tips.

Ask for: "Facts You Need to Know about Gas Supply"
Send: a postcard
To: Entex, Inc.
Sales Dept.
P.O. Box 2628
Houston, TX 77001

GAS
- Gas will heat 2.4 gallons of water with the same amount of primary energy it takes to heat 1 gallon electrically.
- Gas will dry 3-1/3 loads of clothes with the same amount of primary energy it takes to dry 1 load electrically.

Burners

A 12-page pamphlet and a foldout about the burners for gas and oil heaters. Published by the EPA, these bulletins suggest that periodic servicing of burners help maintain safety, save fuel and cut pollution.
- "Get the Most from Your Gas Heating Dollar"
- "Get the Most from Your Heating Oil Dollar"

Ask for: each publication you want by name
Send: a postcard
To: Office of Public Awareness
Mail Drop 50
Environmental Research Ctr.
Research Triangle Park, NC 27711

&EPA Get the Most from Your Heating Oil Dollar
Servicing Cuts Cost and Pollution

Insulation

A foldout about Certainteed fiberglass insulation. The foldout describes the product and provides instructions on how to determine the amount and kind of insulation needed for your attic. Installation tips are also offered. The foldout includes a note about the federal income tax credit available to people installing insulation in their homes.

Ask for: "Insulation Facts Add Up to Energy Savings"
Send: a postcard
To: Certainteed Home Inst.
P.O. Box 860
Valley Forge, PA 19482

Weatherproofing

An easy-to-read, illustrated, 16-page booklet about insulating and weatherproofing your home. The booklet briefly explains insulation materials, r-factor, where and how to install insulation and how to control moisture. It also contains a checklist for preventing air filtration.

Ask for: "Insulate Your Home"
Send: a postcard with name and address
To: Entex, Inc.
Sales Dept.
P.O. Box 2628
Houston, TX 77001

Cellulose

A 4-page brochure on K-19 cellulose insulation. Making your home more energy efficient is the aim of this brochure. This material advocates K-19 insulation as the best choice for year-round comfort. Specifications for installation are included.

Ask for: "K-19 Cellulose Insulation"
Send: a 9" self-addressed, stamped envelope
To: National Cellulose Corp.
Attn.: Dan Kelly (FHH-81)
P.O. Box 45006
Houston, TX 77045

CONDENSATION
An excess accumulation of moisture or condensation in walls, ceilings and floors can be prevented by the following measures:

- Install an approved vapor barrier toward the warm (inside) surface.
- In unheated areas, provide adequate ventilation openings to the outside of the house.

COLD FLOORS
Have you noticed cold walls and floors in your house or patches of snow on the roof? These signs indicate the loss of warm air in an inadequately insulated house. The heat resistance and sealing effects of K-19 insulation help to prevent this heat loss. Warm air is more evenly distributed; floors are warmer.

Saving Energy

Pipe Insulation

A foldout about a type of insulation for water pipes. It explains how this vinyl-clad polyurethane foam insulation is made and presents a chart comparing heat loss from uninsulated pipe to heat loss from this insulated pipe. Another chart shows how this insulation compares to others in density, structure, handling ease, heat stability and more. Includes a free sample of the insulation.

Ask for: "Foamedge Pipe Cover"
Send: 25¢
To: Teledyne Mono-Thane
　　Dept. FS
　　1460 Industrial Pkwy.
　　Akron, OH 44310

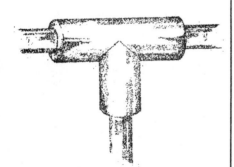

Ventilation

A foldout describing the hows and whys of attic ventilation. Several types of ventilation and their drawbacks are described; following this, the "ridge vent" system, tested by both H.C. Products and the University of Illinois with very positive results, is illustrated.

Ask for: "How and Why Attics Are Ventilated"
Send: a 9″ self-addressed, stamped envelope
To: H.C. Products Co.
　　917 N. Santa Fe Ave.
　　Princeville, IL 61559

COMFORT

If an attic is not ventilated, the summer sun beating down on the roof can heat up the underside of the roof to 160° F. or more. An effective attic ventilation system keeps the attic temperature to within 10 or 15 degrees of the outside air temperature even on the hottest days.

Doors

An 8-page booklet illustrating and explaining the importance of properly installing and insulating wood doors in order to prevent energy loss. Discusses amount of energy lost through doors, wood as an insulating material, wood vs. steel, proper installation of weatherstripping, insulated glass and the aesthetics of wood.

Ask for: "The Facts about Energy and Wood Doors"
Send: 35¢
To: Fir & Hemlock Door Assn.
　　Dept. FH-3
　　Yeon Bldg.
　　Portland, OR 97204

Window Waste

A large foldout about windows and energy for anyone with old or leaking windows. The foldout identifies 3 ways windows waste energy, outlines solutions to each problem and also points out how windows can increase energy efficiency. It describes and illustrates how to install "custom-fit" replacement windows, which can be a significant conservation measure.

Ask for: "Windows and Energy Brochure"
Send: a postcard
To: Season-All
    Indiana, PA 15701

HEAT LOSS
Deteriorated windows in the average 2-story house lose 70% more energy than the ceiling. As the number of floors in a home or building increases, the significance of the ceiling becomes less and less, and the opportunity for energy savings with windows increases. In a 2-story house, the windows lose 170% as much as the ceiling. In a 3-story house, the windows lose 255% as much.

New Windows

A 16-page pamphlet dealing with the replacement of old, worn-out, drafty windows and gliding doors with new quality materials. Before-and-after illustrated examples are discussed and common questions answered.

Ask for: "Introducing Exactly What You Need in a Replacement Window"
Send: a postcard
To: Andersen Corp.
    Dept. L-7
    Bayport, MN 55003

Introducing exactly what you need in a replacement window:

Windows

A 136-page, illustrated booklet about windows – their history, the ways they waste energy and some solutions to those problems. This material gives step-by-step instructions for installing storm windows and replacement windows, describes the new thermalized windows on the market and talks about investment paybacks for various window insulation measures. Quotes from literature about windows are sprinkled throughout.

Ask for: "The Window Book"
Send: $1.00
To: Season-All
    Indiana, PA 15701

LEAKAGE
How do you spot the problems? Start with a simple test. Take a lit candle and, being careful of the shades or drapes, move the candle around the perimeter of the window (where the plaster and the inside casing meet). If the candle flickers, you've got air leakage – not in the window itself, but between the wall and the window.

Saving Energy

Window Ice

A 54-page, easy-to-read, illustrated booklet about windows and moisture condensation. It explains how windows waste energy, details the causes of condensation and ice forming on windows, and suggests ways to minimize or solve the problem. The booklet contains a chart and suggestions to help homeowners diagnose the causes of their condensation problems.

Ask for: "Windows and Condensation"
Send: $1.00
To: Season-All
Indiana, PA 15701

Triple Glazing

An 8-page pamphlet with answers to common questions about triple glazing. Tables help calculate the savings in heating cost and the payback periods, and illustrations describe the installation of various types of triple glazing.

Ask for: "The Andersen Triple Glazing Book"
Send: a postcard
To: Andersen Corp.
Dept. L-14
Bayport, MN 55003

Q & A
What is triple glazing anyway? If the windows in your home have double-pane insulating glass, they have two panes of glass with a sealed air space between them. Triple glazing is the addition of another pane of glass to the outside of the windows.

Wood Windows

A 16-page booklet on wood windows that answers homeowners' most frequent questions. Style, quality, location, energy usage, aesthetic value, care and remodeling are among the topics considered.

Ask for: "A Guide to Energy-Saving Windows"
Send: a postcard
To: National Woodwork Mfrs. Assn.
% SR&A
355 Lexington Ave.
New York, NY 10017

Window Facts

A 16-page pamphlet about the role of windows and sliding doors in energy conservation. Among the topics covered are how to heat with windows, how to save fuel in cold and warm climates and how to shop for energy-efficient doors and windows. Photographs and sketches illustrate how adequate window area can improve a home.

Ask for: "Andersen Energy Facts"
Send: a postcard
To: Andersen Corp.
Dept. L-11
Bayport, MN 55003

COLD CLIMATES

To take advantage of winter solar heat gain November through March, the largest window area should face south, with lesser glass area to the east, west and particularly north. Use double-pane insulating glass or triple glazing to reduce winter conducted heat loss through the glass.

Wood Stoves

A 24-page booklet that primarily deals with the questions consumers have about wood and coal stoves. The fireplace "insert" stove is fully described, with a discussion of its benefits, safety considerations and installation instructions. The booklet also includes freestanding stoves.

Ask for: "Making Sense Out of Wood Stoves and Coal Stoves"
Send: $1.00
To: Hayes Equipment Corp.
P.O. Box 526Z
Unionville, CT 06085

MAKING SENSE OUT OF WOOD STOVES

Better'n Ben's

Wood Heat

A foldout that re-examines some of the assumptions people make when they buy a stove or fireplace to cut fuel costs. The foldout considers the efficiency of fireplaces and stoves and lists ways to make them even more efficient. Also tells how to choose a stove for your purpose and explains the different kinds of stoves.

Ask for: "Wood Stoves and Fireplaces"
Send: a 9″ self-addressed, stamped envelope
To: Information Div.
West Virginia Dept. of Agriculture
Charleston, WV 25305

CAST-IRON STOVES

Cast-iron stoves are the best because cast iron holds up well under heat, has a long life, spreads the heat away from hot spots in the fire, and generally does not warp. However, cast iron cracks easily if dropped. Used cast-iron stoves should be thoroughly inspected by a person knowledgeable in their construction.

Saving Energy

Woodburning Stoves

An informational package on woodburning stoves and their most efficient use in the modern home. Explores considerations for locating a stove and outlines stove types. Gives tips on the best methods for cutting and storing wood.

Ask for: information package
Send: $1.00
To: Energy Harvesters Corp.
P.O. Box 19FS
Fitzwilliam, NH 03447

Wood Stoves

A catalog for the 4 wood-heating stoves made by Kickapoo and for accessories, kerosene lamps and books about heating with wood. The catalog includes illustrations, letters from satisfied customers, fuel values of some common woods and a formula for comparing the cost of heating your home with wood to the cost of your current fuel.

Ask for: catalog
Send: a postcard
To: Kickapoo Stove Works, Ltd.
P.O. Box 127-5F
La Farge, WI 54639

Stove Safety

A foldout for anyone who owns a wood stove or is thinking of buying one. The foldout provides basic information on the selection, installation, use and maintenance of wood-burning stoves. In particular, it reviews guidelines for chimneys and stove pipes and suggests how to prevent potentially dangerous creosote from building up.

Ask for: "Wood Stove Safety"
Send: a postcard
To: Insurance Information Inst.
110 William St. – FS
New York, NY 10038

Energy Harvesters® is a very special design!

KICKAPOO
1980 Catalog

SAFETY TIPS
- Make sure there is enough clearance between the stove and combustible floors, walls and ceilings.
- Place the stove on a fireproof base.
- Have a mason or other competent person inspect the chimney.
- Burn only dry, well-seasoned wood.

Firewood

A foldout on the selection, purchase and use of firewood for your fireplace. Where to get firewood, how to buy it, how to choose the best wood for burning and how to build a better – and a safer – fire are discussed. A table showing the relative efficiency ratings of a variety of dried woods is included.

Ask for: "Firewood for Your Fireplace"
Send: $1.00
To: Consumer Information Ctr.
Dept. 163J
Pueblo, CO 81009

WOOD SELECTION
Soft woods like pine, spruce and fir are easy to ignite and burn rapidly with a hot flame. The heavier hard woods, such as ash, beech, birch, maple and oak, burn less vigorously and with a shorter flame. Aroma comes from the woods of fruit trees, such as apple and cherry and from nut trees, such as beech, hickory and pecan.

Fireplace Accessories

A 32-page, full-color catalog of fireplace furnishings. The catalog lists a wide variety of firescreens and accessories and gives instructions on measuring, ordering and installing your fireplace furnishings. Also includes information on the proper method of selecting and storing wood.

Ask for: "Complete Fireplace Furnishings"
Send: $1.00
To: Portland Willamette Co.
6499 N.E. 59th Pl.
Portland, OR 97218

Fire Tools

A 36-page catalog of fireplace equipment and accessories such as screens, log holders, bellows and fire tools. The catalog also includes many other metal items – everything from bookends and door-knockers to weathervanes. Black-and-white photographs or drawings of every item add to descriptions. A price list is provided.

Ask for: "Lemee's Fireplace Equipment Catatlog"
Send: $1.00
To: Lemee's Fireplace Equipment – C
815 Bedford St.
Bridgewater, MA 02324

BEST BETS
- Flat and folding fireplace screens
- Firesets, with brushes, shovels, forks and pokers
- Andirons
- Brass wood baskets
- Canvas log carriers
- Cast-iron grates
- Matchholders & bellows

Fireplaces

A 24-page, illustrated booklet on fireplaces and chimneys. The construction and maintenance of both chimneys and fireplaces are discussed at length. In addition, the booklet includes helpful information about fireplace design, modified fireplaces, prefabricated fireplaces and chimneys, and outdoor fireplaces.

Ask for: "Fireplaces and Chimneys"
Send: $1.00
To: Consumer Information Ctr.
Dept. 162J
Pueblo, CO 81009

Chimney Care

A 10-page booklet on chimney maintenance. Today, people are using their fireplaces more than ever, and this booklet provides essential information on the details of chimney maintenance. A short history of chimney sweeps is an additional bonus.

Ask for: "For Whatever Soots You"
Send: a postcard
To: August West Systems, Inc.
14 Wilton Rd.
Westport, CT 06880

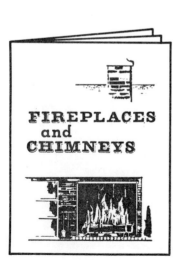

FIREPLACES
and
CHIMNEYS

CLEANING
Don't take your chimney for granted. It's an essential part of your wood-burning system. To keep it functioning properly, have it inspected often and cleaned when dirty. It's a good rule-of-thumb to have a fireplace looked at after every 1 cord; a wood stove that's used regularly should be checked every 6 months.

Books & More

A checklist of books and bulletins of interest to the homeowner. The topics incude energy sources, building, furniture, fireplaces and much more. Ordering information is provided.

Ask for: "Country Wisdom Books and Bulletins"
Send: a postcard
To: Garden Way Publishing
Dept. A564
Charlotte, VT 05445

BEST BETS
- *Your Energy-Efficient House* (Anthony Adams)
- *The Complete Book of Heating with Wood* (Larry Gay)
- *Planning and Building Your Fireplace* (Margaret and Wilbur Eastman, Jr.)
- *Building the House You Can Afford* (Stu Campbell)

Energy Books

A 12-page booklet listing dozens of informational publications on solar and other forms of energy. Included are books and other publications providing information on general energy concepts, building design, use of solar energy, solar conversion, wind energy kits, plans, technical literature and much more.

Ask for: "Solar and Other Sources of Energy Bibliography"
Send: $1.00
To: American Section of Intl. Solar
Energy Society
Research Inst. for Advanced
Technology
W. Hwy. 190
Killeen, TX 76541

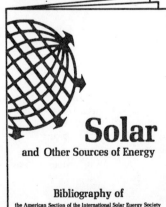

Solar
and Other Sources of Energy

Bibliography of
the American Section of the International Solar Energy Society

Energy Books

A catalog listing over 70 books on solar and other home energy options, such as wind, wood and solid waste. Included are books on energy conservation, technology and the process of designing and constructing homes, buildings and greenhouses. Books contain examples and illustrations, as well as tips on saving energy.

Ask for: "Solar Energy Book Catalog"
Send: a 9" self-addressed, stamped envelope
To: Centerline Co.
Dept. A151
401 S. 36th St.
Phoenix, AZ 85034

BEST BETS
- *Consumer Handbook of Solar Energy* (John H. Keyes)
- *Dome Builder's Handbook* (William Yarnell)
- *Home Energy How To* (A.J. Hand)
- *Homeowner's Guide to Solar Heating & Cooling* (W.M. Foster)

Solar Hotline

The National Solar Heating and Cooling Information Center offers a toll-free telephone number (open Monday through Friday, 9:00 A.M. to 5:00 P.M., in all continental time zones) to answer introductory or technical questions about solar power. Call the Center for free information about solar energy.

Ask for: information
Call: (800) 523-2929 – continental U.S., Puerto Rico and Virgin Islands
(800) 462-4983 – Pennsylvania
(800) 523-4700 – Alaska and Hawaii

**NATIONAL
SOLAR**
HEATING AND COOLING
INFORMATION CENTER
800/523-2929
IN PENNSYLVANIA: 800/462-4983
IN ALASKA, HAWAII: 800/523-4700

Solar Basics

A packet of information (brochures, booklets and bibliographies) describing the basics of solar energy to heat your home and your hot water. Information is included on how the principles of solar energy apply to your home, your climate and your budget.

Ask for: "Solar Information"
Send: a postcard
To: SOLAR
P.O. Box 1607
Rockville, MD 20850

ZONING & TAXES

Before your solar system is installed, be sure your installer checks local building and zoning regulations. Also, find out whether you will gain any tax advantages from owning a solar system; many states and communities have already passed laws which grant a reduction or exemption on sales, income or property taxes to the owners of solar systems.

Solar Digest

A free, sample issue of an illustrated monthly newsletter, *Solar Energy Digest.* It covers all areas of the solar field, including architecture and building, energy storage, hydro, ocean thermal, photovoltaics and more. It also carries features such as book reviews and a calendar of significant meetings, conferences and schools.

Ask for: a sample copy of *Solar Energy Digest*
Send: a 9″ self-addressed, stamped envelope
To: Solar Energy Digest
P.O. Box 17776FS
San Diego, CA 92117

Solar News

A miscellany of solar energy news, reprints, newsletters and other information. Materials are selected from such sources as popular magazines, government publications, professional magazines and the Congressional Record.

Ask for: "Solar Information Packet"
Send: $1.00
To: Thomason Solar Homes, Inc.
609 Cedar Ave.
Fort Washington, MD 20022

SUNPOWER
Is it possible to heat a home with almost no fuel except sunpower during winter in Washington, DC? The answer is yes. There is a solar-heated home in Washington, DC, which does it. It is warm when it is zero degrees outside, warm on days with 6 inches of snow on the ground, warm even on cloudy days. Warm means 72° inside.

Energy Options

A 14-page consumer guide to solar and other alternative forms of energy that describes how these alternatives work and how you can use them in your home. This guide, which is normally available for a $2.00 donation, also considers common energy-wasting practices and suggests ways to cut back on energy consumption.

Ask for: "Solar Lobby's Consumer Guide"
Send: $1.00
To: Consumer Guide
Solar Lobby
1001 Connecticut Ave. NW
Rm. 510FH
Washington, DC 20036

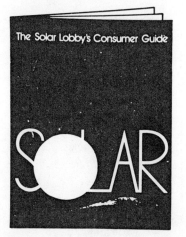

The Solar Lobby's Consumer Guide

SOLAR

Solar Energy

An information-packed foldout providing consumer information on solar energy devices. The foldout describes in some detail the issues a homeowner must consider before installing solar equipment and helps the reader avoid several pitfalls. Included are tips on comparing system features and choosing a contractor.

Ask for: "Don't Get Burned with Solar Energy"
Send: $1.00
To: American Section of Intl. Solar Energy Society
Research Inst. for Advanced Technology
W. Hwy. 190
Killeen, TX 76541

SOME QUESTIONS
If you are considering adding solar to an existing building, ask yourself the following questions: Is your home well insulated? Do you have a roof or wall with sufficient southern exposure? Are the roof and building strong enough to support the equipment? Is your present heating system compatible? Will your homeowner's insurance premiums increase?

Solar Poster

A full-color, 24″ x 29″ poster that depicts a sunset over wheat fields and pastures. The caption reads "Solar/Renewable Energy." This poster makes an attractive wall decoration in addition to spreading the word about solar energy.

Ask for: "Solar/Renewable Energy Poster" (#EDM-848 – color)
Send: a postcard
To: Energy
    P.O. Box 62
    Oak Ridge, TN 37830

Solar System

A foldout and 3 handouts about a solar system that does not need to have a southern exposure and that operates in all weather conditions – sunshine, rain, clouds, wind and after sundown. The foldout explains the system's advantages and how it works. Included are photographs, engineering specifications and suggested retail-price list.

Ask for: "Subambient Solar Systems, including SSI, Sunbrat and Windstar models"
Send: a postcard
To: Solar Specialties, Inc.
    Rte. 7, P.O. Box 409
    Golden, CO 80401

ADVANTAGES
- Low cost
- Easily installed in new or older homes
- House can be oriented in any direction
- Unbreakable collectors that contain no glass
- Operates efficiently during rainy, snowy and cloudy weather.

Solar Supplies

An informative, 64-page catalog of components and equipment for solar energy systems (both passive and active). A newsletter, a sample of Sunlite collector cover material, a price list and order forms are inserted.

Ask for: "Kalwall Solar Components, Do-It-Yourself Solar Heating and Supply-Shop and Mail-Order Warehouse"
Send: $1.00
To: Solar Components
    Free Stuff Dept.
    P.O. Box 237
    Manchester, NH 03105

State Energy Agencies

Each state, plus the District of Columbia, has an agency or department that handles consumers' energy questions. You can contact your state agency with virtually any question you have: how to arrange for an energy audit, what tax credits are available if you install a solar system, how to insulate your home, etc. And most agencies distribute free publications and will refer you to other state departments or private organizations that will try to assist you. Write or call the energy department in your state – many have toll-free hotline numbers.

Alabama
Alabama Dept. of Energy
3734 Atlanta Hwy.
Montgomery, AL 36130
(800) 392-8098

Alaska
Alaska Div. of Energy &
  Power Development
338 Denali
Anchorage, AK 99501

Arizona
Arizona Energy Office
1700 W. Washington
5th Floor
Phoenix, AZ 85007
(800) 532-5499

Arkansas
Public Outreach
State Energy Office
3000 Kavanaugh St.
Little Rock, AR 72205
(800) 482-1122

California
California Energy Commission
1111 Howe Ave.
Sacramento, CA 95825
(800) 852-7516

Colorado
Colorado Dept. of Energy
1525 Sherman
Denver, CO 80203

Connecticut
Public Information Unit
Energy Div.
80 Washington St.
Hartford, CT 06115
(800) 842-1648

Delaware
Delaware Energy Office
56 The Green
Dover, DE 19901
(800) 282-8616

District of Columbia
District of Columbia Energy Unit
1420 N. York Ave. NW
Washington, DC 20005

Florida
Governor's Energy Office
301 Bryant Bldg.
Tallahassee, FL 32301

Georgia
Georgia Office of Energy
  Resources
270 Washington St., SW
Atlanta, GA 30334

Hawaii
State Energy Office
Dept. of Planning & Economic
  Development
1164 Bishop St.
Honolulu, HI 96813

Idaho
Idaho Office of Energy
State House
Boise, ID 83720

Illinois
Illinois Inst. of Natural Resources
325 W. Adams St.
Springfield, IL 62706

Indiana
Energy Office Group
Indiana Dept. of Commerce
440 N. Meridian
Indianapolis, IN 46204

Iowa
Iowa Energy Policy Council
Lucas Bldg.
Des Moines, IA 50319
(800) 532-1114

Saving Energy

Kansas
Kansas Energy Office
214 W. 6th St.
Topeka, KS 66603
(800) 432-3537

Kentucky
Kentucky Dept. of Energy
P.O. Box 11888
Lexington, KY 40578

Louisiana
Dept. of Natural Resources
P.O. Box 44156
Baton Rouge, LA 70804

Maine
Office of Energy Res.
295 Water St., Sta. 53
Augusta, ME 04333

Maryland
Maryland Energy Policy Office
301 W. Preston
Baltimore, MD 21201
(800) 492-5903

Massachusetts
Executive Office of Energy
  Resources
73 Tremont St.
Boston, MA 02108
(800) 922-8265

Michigan
Energy Administration
Michigan Dept. of Commerce
P.O. Box 30228
Lansing, MI 48910

Minnesota
Minnesota Energy Agency
150 E. Kellogg Blvd.
St. Paul, MN 55101
(800) 292-4704

Mississippi
Mississippi Dept. of Energy &
  Transportation
Watkins Bldg.
510 George St.
Jackson, MS 39202

Missouri
Energy Information Clearing
  House
Missouri Div. of Energy
1915 South Ridge Dr.
Jefferson City, MO 65101
(800) 392-0717

Montana
Natural Resources & Conservation
  Dept.
Energy Div.
32 S. Ewing
Helena, MT 59620

Nebraska
Nebraska Energy Office
P.O. Box 95085
Lincoln, NB 68509

Nevada
Nevada Dept. of Energy
400 W. King St.
Carson City, NV 89710

New Hampshire
Education & Outreach Office
Governor's Council on Energy
2½ Beacon St.
Concord, NH 03301
(800) 852-3466

New Jersey
New Jersey Dept. of Energy
Office of Conservation
101 Commerce St.
Newark, NJ 07102
(800) 492-4242

New Mexico
Office of Secretary
Energy & Mining Dept.
P.O. Box 2770
Santa Fe, NM 87501
(800) 432-6782

New York
State Energy Office
2 Rockefeller Plaza
Albany, NY 12223
(800) 342-3722

North Carolina
Energy Div.
North Carolina Dept. of Commerce
P.O. Box 25249
Raleigh, NC 27611
(800) 662-7131

North Dakota
Energy Management &
  Conservation
1533 N. 12th St.
State Capitol Bldg.
Bismarck, ND 58501

Ohio
Ohio Dept. of Energy
30 E. Broad St.
Columbus, OH 43215
(800) 282-9234

Oklahoma
Oklahoma Dept. of Energy
4400 N. Lincoln Blvd.
Oklahoma City, OK 73105

Oregon
Oregon Dept. of Energy
102 Labor & Industry Bldg.
Salem, OR 97310
(800) 452-7813

Pennsylvania
Governor's Energy Council
P.O. Box 8010
Harrisburg, PA 17105
(800) 882-8400

Rhode Island
Rhode Island Energy Office
80 Dean St.
Providence, RI 02903

South Carolina
Governor's Div. of Energy
  Resources
1122 Lady St.
Columbia, SC 29201

South Dakota
Office of Energy Policy
Capitol Lake Plaza
Pierre, SD 57501
(800) 592-1865

Tennessee
Energy Information Center
Tennessee Energy Authority
Conservation Section
Capitol Blvd.
Nashville, TN 37219
(800) 342-1340

Texas
Texas Energy & Natural Resource
  Advisory Council
200 E. 18th St.
Austin, TX 78701

Utah
Utah Energy Office
231 E. 400 St.
Salt Lake City, UT 84111

Vermont
State Energy Office
State Office Bldg.
Montpelier, VT 05602

Virginia
State Office of Emergency &
  Energy Services
310 Turner Rd.
Richmond, VA 23225
(800) 552-3831

Washington
State Energy Office
400 E. Union St.
Olympia, WA 98504

West Virginia
West Virginia Fuel & Energy Office
1591 Washington St. E
Charleston, WV 25311
(800) 642-9012

Wisconsin
Division of State Energy
101 S. Webster
Madison, WI 53702

Wyoming
Wyoming Energy Conservation
  Office
Capitol Hill Office Bldg.
Cheyenne, WY 82002
(800) 442-6783

Decorating & Improving

Furniture

Two large and attractive catalogs of bedroom and dining-room furniture. The first, "The Whitehall Collection," contains pieces based on 18th-century English designs. The second, "Lorraine V," features French Provincial furniture. Also included is a booklet that describes how White's furniture is made and how you can care for it.

Ask for: "The Whitehall Collection" and "Lorraine V"
Send: 50¢
To: White Furniture Co.
Dept. M
P.O. Box 367
Mebane, NC 27302

Early American

The current edition (plus 3 future issues) of the Sturbridge Yankee Workshop catalog of early American furniture, decorating items, collectibles and gift items. Includes prints, lamps, linens, curtains, bath accessories, china, figurines and gourmet utensils. All items are absolutely guaranteed, and a mail-order form is included.

Ask for: "Sturbridge Yankee Workshop Catalog"
Send: 50¢
To: Sturbridge Yankee Workshop
742 Brimfield Turnpike
Sturbridge, MA 01566

BEST BETS
- Personalized stained glass windows
- Limited-edition porcelain dolls
- Reproduction of a slat-top Lay's desk, circa 1740
- English Staffordshire Blue Willow pattern china
- Weathervanes in 21 designs

Pine Furniture

A colorful 84-page catalog of quality pine furniture and accessories. Furniture in a wide variety of styles – from the simplicity of the Shaker collection to classic Queen Anne and unusual Chinoiserie – is available. Unique gifts and Christmas items are also included. An order form is provided.

Ask for: "Yield House Catalog"
Send: a postcard
To: Yield House Inc.
Dept. MPO1
Attn.: Jill Bigelow
Rte. 16
North Conway, NH 03860

Country Bed

A foldout describing the traditional pencil post bed. Pencil post beds are a classic American form, available in a variety of styles. The beds can be used with either traditional rope springs or with the modern box spring. Descriptions, illustrations, ordering information and an order form are included.

Ask for: "The Pencil Post Bed"
Send: 30¢ (in stamps or coin)
To: The Country Bed Shop
   North Main
   Groton, MA 01450

Kids' Rooms

A 20-page booklet with a variety of suggestions for decorating children's rooms. The importance of selecting furniture that will "grow" with children is stressed, and room size, color, texture and division are taken into account. Room descriptions and full color photographs are included to aid planning.

Ask for: "Children's Rooms"
Send: $1.00
To: The Furniture Family
   Attn.: Dept. FSC
   Box 1504
   Lexington, NC 27292

Home Catalog

An information-packed, 160-page catalog of products to help with do-it-yourself projects to improve your home. The catalog features products for home exteriors, interiors, bath, kitchen, lawn and garden. It offers paint, wallpaper, floor coverings, home security, kitchen cabinets, light fixtures and much more.

Ask for: "Sears Home Improvement Catalog"
Send: a postcard
To: Sears, Roebuck and Co.
   Dept. 703, BSC 40-15
   Sears Tower
   Chicago, IL 60684

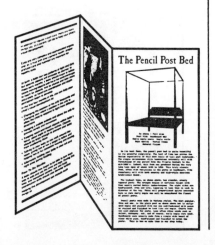

Decorating & Improving

Remodeling

A 28-page, step-by-step handbook on kitchen remodeling. Includes sections on analyzing your kitchen needs, buying appliances, solving storage problems and selecting a contractor, plus design options, do-it-yourself decorating ideas and tips on safety and kitchen care. Also includes a graph to sketch a rough design of the kitchen plan you want.

Ask for: "Kitchen Remodeling"
Send: $1.00
To: Kitchen Remodeling
274 Brannan St.
San Francisco, CA 94107

Kitchen Guide

A 12-page booklet for those interested in remodeling their kitchens. The guide illustrates 4 basic kitchen arrangements, discusses cabinet selection and placement, answers common questions and provides a planning graph and a step-by-step guide for cabinet installation.

Ask for: "Do-It-Yourself Kitchen Guide"
Send: 50¢
To: Haas Cabinet Co., Inc.
625 W. Utica St.
Sellersburg, IN 47172

Kitchen Decor

A full-color, 8-page booklet on "Quick Change Dishwasher Decorating." This do-it-yourself booklet suggests making the front of your dishwasher a decorating focal point. Five decorating styles are illustrated, and decorating suggestions are offered for cabinets, countertops, walls, floors, furnishings and accessories, as well as the dishwasher itself.

Ask for: "Quick Change Dishwasher Decorating"
Send: 50¢
To: Consumer Information Ctr.
The Maytag Co.
Newton, IA 50208

Kitchen & Bath

A 16-page, full-color pamphlet on planning your ideal kitchen or bath. Efficient "work-triangles," storage considerations, cabinet selection and "ten tips to a happy ending" are all outlined.

Ask for: "Kitchen and Bath Planning"
Send: 35¢
To: National Kitchen Cabinet Assn.
Dept. CM
P.O. Box 2978, Grand Central Sta.
New York, NY 10017

A FEW TIPS
- Install enough electrical outlets above countertops for small appliances and health and beauty equipment.
- Install good, non-glare lighting above kitchen work centers.
- Use wall-hung toilets in bathrooms. They're easier to clean around than floor-based models.

Kitchen Design

Two directories published by the American Institute of Kitchen Dealers that list the names and addresses of kitchen designers, retailers, distributors and manufacturers – all of whom are certified to be well-trained, competent and fair. Each over 60 pages long, the directories are arranged alphabetically by state and by city to make it easy to find those in your area.

Ask for: "Directory of Certified Kitchen Designers" and "Directory of Accredited Members"
Send: a postcard
To: Ray W. Afflerbach, CKD
AIKD – FS Directories
124 Main St.
Hackettstown, NJ 07840

Bath Ideas

A 40-page catalog of bathroom, powder room and kitchen fixtures. Filled with gorgeous color photographs of elegantly designed rooms, this catalog offers ideas to anyone designing or remodeling a home. Includes whirlpool baths, spas, environmental enclosures, shower coves, bidets, decorative faucets and much more.

Ask for: "Kohler Elegance: Great Ideas for Bathrooms, Powder Rooms and Kitchens"
Send: $1.00
To: Kohler Co.
P.O. Box FS
Kohler, WI 53044

NOSTALGIA
- Turn-of-the-century vintage toilet with elevated tank, pull-down chain, oak seat and cover.
- Birthday bath with rolled rim, ball-and-claw feet.
- Continentally styled Chablis pedestal lavatory.
- "Antique" faucets.

Decorating & Improving

Tile

A 16-page catalog offering handmade tile products for residential and commercial use. Includes both glazed and unglazed tiles, ranging from solid colors to intricate designs. Also offers handmade sinks, accessories, coordinated bathrooms, precast pavers, lava stone tiles and marble tiles.

Ask for: catalog
Send: a postcard
To: Elon, Inc.
150 E. 58th St.
New York, NY 10022

Window Fashions

An 8-page catalog of assorted window fashions. Shutters, fabric frames, woven wood, bamboo shades, Danish shades and various types of blinds and draperies are available. Helpful instructions for measuring are included.

Ask for: "The World of Window Fashions"
Send: a postcard
To: Perkowitz Window Fashions
Dept. FSH
135 Green Bay Rd.
Wilmette, IL 60091

Roman Shades

An information sheet on how to make and use the Roman shade. A list of the necessary materials and detailed instructions for making the shades are included. These shades can be inexpensive or elegant and can be used in any room in the house. They can be lowered to shut out light or raised to control light and let in a view.

Ask for: "How to Make and Use the Roman Shade" (I.S. 321)
Send: a postcard
To: Ms. Nancy B. Sweet, Pub. Editor
P.O. Box 5404MSU
Mississippi Coop. Extension Service
Mississippi State, MS 39762

SHADES
Transparent sun shades are "sunglasses" for your windows and patio doors. Solar heat, glare and fading rays are blocked, yet you will have the full view. Tortoise-shell bamboo shades provide a dramatic effect and are versatile enough to use with many types of decor.

Entry Doors

A full-color foldout describing all the details you need to know about entry doors. Ten styles of doors are illustrated, and information is provided on the care, fitting, hanging, finishing and weatherstripping of entry doors.

Ask for: "Entry Door Brochure"
Send: a postcard
To: E.A. Nord Co.
P.O. Box 1187
Everett, WA 98206

Using Color

A 7-page booklet that suggests ways to use color in home decorating. Includes a color wheel to demonstrate the effects of using contrasting, neighboring or monochromatic colors. The booklet also contains many useful decorating tips as well as 2 full pages of color samples.

Ask for: "Decorate Your Way with Fulcolor®"
Send: 50¢
To: Fuller-O'Brien Paints
Advertising Dept.
450 E. Grand Ave.
South San Franciso, CA 94080

Interiors

A 12-page, full-color booklet on redwood interiors and a large foldout on paneling a room with redwood lumber. The booklet suggests a wide variety of ways to enhance the beauty of your home through the use of redwood, while the foldout provides detailed information on paneling a room.

Ask for: "Redwood Interiors" and "Panel a Room with Redwood Lumber"
Send: 60¢
To: Redwood Interiors
Dept. STUFF
California Redwood Assn.
One Lombard St.
San Francisco, CA 94111

SPACE IDEAS
- Soft, light shades make a small room seem larger, a low ceiling appear higher. Woodwork should match the walls to avoid a cluttered appearance.
- Next thing to sunshine for a dark room is a pretty shade of yellow. This basically warm color is especially attractive in rooms with northern or eastern exposure.

Decorating & Improving

Paneling Tips

An information sheet on "how to panel a room without climbing the walls." Starting **before** the work begins, it explains how to choose the necessary tools, estimate the number of panels needed, prepare the surfaces and deal with uneven walls. A foldout about decorative brick is also available.

Ask for: "How to Panel a Room without Climbing the Walls" and "Towne 'n Country Decorative Brick"
Send: a 9" self-addressed, stamped envelope
To: H.B. Fuller Co.
Attn.: Pam Kelter
315 S. Hicks Rd.
Palatine, IL 60067

ONE AT A TIME
Do one room at a time. This seems self-evident, but people sometimes have the impulse to start in on a second room before finishing the one they're working on. If you get that impulse, lie down until it goes away. Get the one room done completely; then, no matter what happens, you're finished with it. Rome was built one step at a time.

Paneling

A 28-page booklet that provides a complete guide to installing wallpaneling. Selection, preliminaries, installation, unusual surfaces and troublesome construction are discussed and illustrated. Attractive color photographs demonstrate the many ways paneling can enhance a home.

Ask for: "The Paneling Book"
Send: $1.00
To: Dept. FSH/Advertising Dept.
Georgia-Pacific Corp.
900 S.W. Fifth Ave.
Portland, OR 97204

THE PANELING BOOK
Complete Guide to Installing Wall Paneling

How to Panel Normal and "Problem" Walls, Arches and Alcoves, Stair Walls and More Plus Great Decorating Ideas

Georgia-Pacific

Plaster Wallpaper

Four pages about and a small sample of Flexi-Wall, a heavy, jute-reinforced "plaster wallpaper." Best described as a patented "plaster in a roll," Flexi-Wall can be used to give old walls of all sorts a new appearance. A description, technical data and installation instructions are included.

Ask for: "Flexi-Wall Plaster in a Roll"
Send: a 9" self-addressed, stamped envelope
To: Flexi-Wall Systems
Dept. FSH
P.O. Box 88
Liberty, SC 29657

MAINTENANCE
The longevity of Flexi-Wall finish can be expected to equal or exceed conventional plaster. The carefully graded quality gypsum used in Flexi-Wall rolled plaster provides a tight, nonporous surface into which dirt and grime cannot easily penetrate. Except for an occasional washing with mild soap and water, no maintenance is required.

Wall Shingles

An 8-page booklet that shows decorating ideas for interior walls using red cedar shingles or handsplit shakes. Color photographs of both residential and commercial applications are included. Step-by-step information on how to apply these materials is shown, along with pictures and specifications of available styles and grades.

Ask for: "Superior Interiors"
Send: 35¢
To: Franklin C. Welch
Red Cedar Shingle & Handsplit Shake Bureau
515 116th Ave. NE, Ste. 275
Bellevue, WA 98004

Wallcoverings

An illustrated, 15-page booklet about wallpapering. The booklet thoroughly explains how to choose wallcoverings to suit your taste and the room, how to measure and buy the covering and how to hang it. A list and drawings of tools you'll need, a chart for figuring out how much wallcovering to buy and a glossary of terms are included.

Ask for: "All You Need To Know about Wallcoverings"
Send: 50¢
To: All About Wallcoverings
P.O. Box 359
66 Morris Ave.
Springfield, NJ 07081

TIPS
- If walls are bumpy, ceiling lines uneven, or there are similar architectural faults, stay away from stripes or other straight-line designs, shiny Mylar or plain wallcoverings.
- Consider minor wall conditions. Embossed textures and all-over pattern designs can hide a multitude of sins.

Wallcoverings

A catalog of wallcoverings, including vinyls, prepasted styles and photo murals, as well as regular papers. The catalog contains 7" x 9" samples of many coverings, with decorating hints, price per roll, size, matching instructions and order numbers on the back of each. Color photographs of the other patterns are included.

Ask for: "Robinson Catalog"
Send: 50¢
To: Robinson's Wallcoverings
Dept. 6DD
225 W. Spring St.
Titusville, PA 16354

Decorating & Improving

Prints

A color catalog of moderately priced, limited-edition prints. Prints are signed and numbered by the artist, and each is custom framed and accompanied by a certificate of authenticity as well as a money-back guarantee. The prints, by artists such as Miró, Chagall and Vasarely, include etchings, lithographs and serigraphs.

Ask for: "Original Print Collectors Group Catalog"
Send: $1.00
To: Original Print Collectors Group
Dept. MP-1
215 Lexington Ave.
New York, NY 10016

Original print collectors group, Ltd.
VOLUME VIII NUMBER 5

Historical Posters

A 16-page catalog offering 600 reproductions of posters, handbills, broadsides, prints and advertisements of historical interest. The reproductions range from America's colonial era to the recent past, including such topics as the Revolutionary War, slavery, new inventions, medicine, circuses, movies and much more.

Ask for: catalog
Send: 50¢
To: Buck Hill Assoc.
Dept. FSH
Garnet Lake Rd.
Johnsburg, NY 12843

BEST BETS
- $1,000 U.S. banknote from 1840
- Vaudeville playbill from 1883
- Eyesight restorer ad
- Flapper styles from 1925
- Laurel & Hardy poster from early film

Picture Frames

A 12-page booklet on do-it-yourself picture framing. The information covers suggested moulding patterns, tools, construction, finishing, matting, liners, mounting, backing, grouping and hanging. Illustrations are included to demonstrate various steps in the process.

Ask for: "Fun-to-Make Picture Frames"
Send: 60¢
To: Wood Moulding and Millwork Producers
Dept. MP
P.O. Box 25278
Portland, OR 97225

FUN-TO-MAKE PICTURE FRAMES

Wood Mouldings

Four publications with detailed descriptions and illustrations of various types of wood mouldings that can be used to decorate your home. The first publication gives installation instructions; the other three offer decorating tips.

- **"How to Work with Wood Mouldings"** (50¢)
- **"Wood Mouldings and Millwork"** (50¢)
- **"Design and Decorate with Wood Mouldings"** (75¢)
- **"American Colonial"** (50¢)

Ask for: each publication you want by name
Send: the appropriate amount for each publication
To: Wood Moulding & Millwork Producers
P.O. Box 25278
Portland, OR 97225

Mouldings & Ornaments

An illustrated, 26-page catalog of wood mouldings and ornaments. This catalog includes carved hardwood, scalloped, overlay and embossed mouldings. The pictured ornaments are also either carved or embossed. Sample cuts are available. Leaflets showing metallic picture frames also come with the catalog.

Ask for: "Wood Mouldings and Ornaments Catalog"
Send: $1.00
To: Joel J. Dorne
Bendix Mouldings, Inc.
235 Pegasus Ave.
Northvale, NJ 07647

Oak Flooring

An 8-page pamphlet on do-it-yourself, solid oak parquet floor covering. The floor covering is described, and step-by-step illustrated instructions explain its installation. Samples of the 3 available colors are also provided.

Ask for: "Hartco Do-It-Yourself Brochure"
Send: a 9″ self-addressed, stamped envelope
To: Hartco
    Dept. FSH – Marketing
    P.O. Drawer A
    Oneida, TN 37841

Hardwood Floors

An 8-page booklet on the installation of hardwood floors. Various methods of installation are discussed and detailed instructions included. Illustrations are used to provide additional information. The use of strip oak flooring on walls and ceilings is also considered.

Ask for: "Hardwood Floor Installation Manual"
Send: 50¢
To: Mr. H. F. Fingerman
    Oak Flooring Inst.
    804 Sterick Bldg.
    Memphis, TN 38103

Floor Ideas

Two short pamphlets on decorating and remodeling. The remodeling pamphlet covers general information, such as working with or without a contractor, selecting products and planning. The decorating pamphlet pays more specific attention to the best ways in which flooring can enhance a home.

Ask for: "Decorating with the Floor in Mind" and "Remodeling with the Floor in Mind"
Send: 50¢
To: Mannington
    Consumer Booklets Dept.
    P.O. Box 30
    Salem, NJ 08079

NEW OVER OLD
When laying a new strip floor over an old floor, the existing wood floor can serve as a subfloor. Drive down any raised nails, renail loose boards and replace any warped boards that can't be made level. Sweep and clean the floor well, but don't use water. Always install the new floor at right angles to the old floor boards.

Books

An informative, 14-page catalog of books for homeowners. Many of the books are about how to do it yourself – everything from plumbing to building a house. The catalog shows each book's cover and describes its purpose and contents, length, price and more. Shipping information and order form are included.

Ask for: "Catalog of Books for the Homeowner"
Send: 25¢
To: Structures Publishing
Dept. MP
P.O. Box 1002
Farmington, MI 48024

Useful Books

A catalog of "how-to" books from Creative Homeowner Press that includes books on bathrooms, kitchens, plumbing systems, fireplaces and patios, as well as 2 books full of home plans. The catalog describes each book at length and gives brief excerpts from each book.

Ask for: "Creative Homeowner Press Catalog"
Send: a postcard
To: Creative Homeowner Press
Dept. F
2266 N. Prospect Ave., #410
Milwaukee, WI 53202

Easy-to-Build

A 20-page booklet describing 10 easy-to-build projects using cut-to-size materials. The projects included are: a plant stand, a stereo unit, a bathroom vanity, a room divider, an appliance center, a modular storage system, a serving cart, a sofa, a workbench and an outdoor chair. A list of materials and illustrated instructions for each project are provided.

Ask for: "Redi-Cuts"
Send: 25¢
To: Dept. FSH/Advertising Dept.
Georgia-Pacific Corp.
900 S.W. Fifth Ave.
Portland, OR 97204

BEST BETS
- *Home Additions* (Joseph F. Schram)
- *Homeowner's Tools* (James Ritchie)
- *Building Primer* (Robert L. Taylor)
- *Home Electrical Wiring* (Larry Mueller)

BEST BETS
- *Home Remodeling Design & Plans* (Herb Hughes)
- *Cabinets & Bookcases* (Tom Philbin)
- *Fireplaces* (Robert E. Jones)
- *Modern Plumbing for Old and New Houses* (Jay Hedden)

Redi-Cuts
Ten easy to build projects using cut-to-size materials.

Improvements

Five foldouts offering plans for a variety of home improvement projects you can build yourself. Each plan provides a materials list, building hints and complete blueprints for the project. Also available is a catalog of over 50 plans you can buy.

- "Built-In Bar"
- "Wheel-About Stereo Stand"
- "Entertainment Center"
- "Plywood Sauna"
- "Slip Together Bed/Desk"
- "Handy Plan Catalog"

Ask for: each publication you want by name
Send: $1.00 for **each**
To: American Plywood Assn.
 Office Services Dept.
 P.O. Box 11700
 Tacoma, WA 98411

Room Divider

A 2-page guide to the construction of a freestanding wall. This easy-to-build wall is the perfect divider for children's rooms: separate them into activity and sleep areas. Photographs show the completed wall and a detailed illustration explains how to build it.

Ask for: "Divide and Conquer with a Freestanding Wall" (X773A)
Send: 75¢
To: Popular Mechanics
 Dept. MP
 P.O. Box 1014, Radio City Sta.
 New York, NY 10101

Veneers

A 14-page booklet explaining a new iron-on veneering technique. The booklet also includes 30 different colors of veneers that can be ordered, plus multicolored inlay bands and artistic inlays and overlays. Instructions for ironing with a hot melt glue sheet are fully explained, as is bonding the veneer to wood with contact cement.

Ask for: "Veneer Craft"
Send: 25¢
To: Bob Morgan Woodworking
Supplies
1123 Bardstown Rd.
Louisville, KY 40204

Spindles

A full-color foldout on spindles and accessories. Styles and sizes of spindles are illustrated, with descriptions of accessories (such as spindle rails and spacers). Also includes information on installation. Fifteen ideas to get you started with spindles are provided.

Ask for: "Spindle Brochure"
Send: a postcard
To: E.A. Nord Co.
P.O. Box 1187
Everett, WA 98206

Plywood Basics

A 61-page booklet, called the "Plywood Encyclopedia." From "acoustical characteristics" to "'Z' flashing," everything you wanted to know about plywood is here. Illustrations and charts supplement basic descriptions of plywood and plywood-related materials.

Ask for: "Plywood Encyclopedia"
Send: $1.00
To: American Plywood Assn.
Office Services Dept.
P.O. Box 11700
Tacoma, WA 98411

BOB MORGAN'S 1980 VENEER CRAFT CATALOG

ANNOUNCING! NEW VENEERING BREAKTHROUGH. USE A HOME IRON AND BOB MORGAN'S HOT MELT GLUE SHEET TO IRON VENEER IN PLACE.

USING SPINDLES
- as candlesticks
- as banisters
- as balcony railings
- as room dividers
- as bed posts
- as window grilles
- in bookshelves

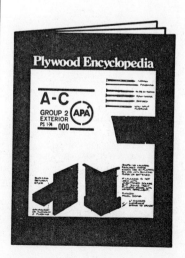

Plywood Encyclopedia

A-C
GROUP 2
EXTERIOR
PS 1-74
000

Decorating & Improving

Plywood

A 12-page booklet that thoroughly describes what plywood is – both for the uninitiated and for those who would like to know more. The booklet covers plywood construction, its history, its advantages over solid lumber, the process of manufacturing it, and the types, grades and sizes of plywood available.

Ask for: "The Story of Hardwood Plywood"
Send: 50¢
To: HPMA
    Literature Request Dept. T
    P.O. Box 2789
    Reston, VA 22090

ADVANTAGES
Plywood manufacturing achieves a more complete utilization of the log than does lumber manufacturing. This is particularly true when comparing the yield of rotary-cut veneer with lumber. No sawdust results from either rotary cutting or slicing, which are the 2 usual methods of cutting veneer.

Plywood

An illustrated 15-page booklet that home carpenters and builders will find useful. It explains the quality criteria for the main types, grades and sizes of hardwood and decorative plywood. The booklet also includes definitions of trade terms and methods of ordering, testing and identifying plywood products, along with detailed charts and illustrations.

Ask for: "NBS Voluntary Product Standard, PS 51-71"
Send: 50¢
To: HPMA
    Literature Request Dept. T
    P.O. Box 2789
    Reston, VA 22090

A Voluntary Standard
Developed by Producers,
Distributors, and Users
With the Cooperation of the
National Bureau of Standards

**Hardwood
and
Decorative
Plywood**

Nails & Gadgets

A 16-page catalog of goods sold by the Tremont Nail Company, including door knockers, cabinet hardware, iron brackets and hinges, dollhouse furniture, kitchen gadgets, novelty items, books about New England crafts and all kinds of antique nails. The catalog also describes the histories of the company and of nail making.

Ask for: "Catalog of General Merchandise"
Send: a postcard
To: Tremont Nail Co.
    Dept. FS
    P.O. Box 111
    Wareham, MA 02571

Housekeeping

Housekeeping

Management

A foldout attacking the housecleaning problem logically with an array of suggestions to help you get more accomplished in less time. Includes tips on tackling jobs efficiently, lightening the workload, managing time and reducing clutter. Helps the reader re-evaluate cleaning standards, task priorities, scheduling and more.

Ask for: "Prescription for Home Management"
Send: a postcard
To: Electrolux Inst. of Home
　　　Management
　　　Dept. MP
　　　P.O. Box 1434
　　　Stamford, CT 06905

GETTING ORGANIZED
Cleaning tasks can be made easier by keeping cleaning supplies together in a portable container or near where they are needed in larger homes. Keeping cleaning tools in good working order and alternating jobs you don't like with those you do like can provide a psychological advantage.

Maintenance

A long and useful booklet on home maintenance. The booklet lists the main areas to watch – the central utility systems, the structure of the building and special problems such as moisture and pest control. It also warns against possible problems in each area and suggests steps to take if these arise. Full of sensible tips.

Ask for: "Protecting Your Housing Investment"
Send: a postcard
To: Consumer Information Ctr.
　　　Dept. 627J
　　　Pueblo, CO 81009

Protecting
Your
Housing Investment

Cleaning

An 18-page pamphlet of housekeeping tips for the hurried. The pamphlet points out the importance of an organized, well-stocked cleaning closet, including a vacuum cleaner that can help with hand chores as well as floors. Offers tips on housekeeping strategies, quick cleaning when entertaining on short notice and choosing the best vacuum cleaner for your needs.

Ask for: "Cleaning on the Run"
Send: 10¢ and a 9″ self-addressed, stamped envelope
To: The Eureka Co.
　　　Dept. COR
　　　Bloomington, IL 60171

CLOSET HELPERS
- Clean rags made from worn-out clothing, sheets, towels and chamois – for all your dusting and polishing chores.
- Baking soda – to clean glass, wall tile and porcelain enamel.
- Peg board – for hanging tools, such as brooms and mops.

Housekeeping

A 10-page pamphlet of helpful hints for homemakers. It includes time- and money-saving tips, suitcase-packing advice, decorating ideas and much more. Specific subjects range from pots and pans and gardening equipment to laundry, children's clothing and closets.

Ask for: "Creative Homemaking"
Send: a postcard
To: Texize
Consumer Relations Dept.,
Box HO
P.O. Box 368
Greenville, SC 29602

Home Care

A 35-page booklet for housekeeping novices and people interested in tips on how to clean and maintain their homes thoroughly but quickly. Thirteen chapters cover everything from cleaning furniture to controlling insects. The booklet also includes a checklist of cleaning tools and supplies essential for regular home care.

Ask for: "Home Care"
Send: a postcard
To: Johnson Wax
Consumer Services Ctr.
P.O. Box 567 – Dept. HOH
Racine, WI 53401

Scratches

Two pages of information on the best methods of repairing scratches in furniture. Common problems discussed include alcohol and other liquids, minor burns and candle wax. The proper care of plastic laminate furniture, plus basic do's and don'ts, are also included.

Ask for: "How to Repair Scratches in Furniture" (X297A)
Send: 75¢
To: Popular Mechanics
Dept. MP
P.O. Box 1014, Radio City Sta.
New York, NY 10101

COOKWARE
- Do not let gas flames lick up the side of pots and pans – it could cause heat stains.
- Do not use metal or enameled cookware to store food as pans may be damaged by salt and acids.
- Remove stuck-on food by pouring cold water into the pan and letting it stand until the food is soft.
- Remove burnt-on food by boiling water in the pan.

TIPS
- Music helps set the mood and creates a pleasant atmosphere. Play a favorite record album or tape while working. A fast Sousa march can help speed up even the most routine chores!
- A clean filter on the air conditioner or furnace means less dust and dirt in the air. Include changing or cleaning filters as part of the regular cleaning schedule.

Reprinted with permission of Johnson Wax.

SOME TIPS
Do immediately remove spilled liquids using a blotting rather than wiping action. Do use only polishes recommended for furniture. Do work with the grain of the wood whether washing, cleaning, polishing or waxing. Don't use nail-polish remover on furniture. Don't wash painted furniture too frequently.

Floor Care

A 16-page pamphlet on the care of wood floors. Types of finish are described and appropriate care discussed. Basic care, stain removal, special surfaces such as distressed wood, cracks, squeaks and refinishing are the other featured topics.

Ask for: "Wood Floor Care Guide"
Send: 25¢
To: Mr. H.F. Fingerman
Oak Flooring Inst.
804 Sterick Bldg.
Memphis, TN 38103

STAIN REMOVAL
• Oil and grease stains: Rub on a kitchen soap having a high lye content, or saturate cotton with hydrogen peroxide and place over stain; then saturate a second layer of cotton with ammonia and place over the first. Repeat until the stain is removed.

Carpets

Four pages of useful information on cleaning and repairing carpets. Basic instructions and complete illustrations demonstrate repairing surface burns, patching, seaming and cleaning. An evaluation of a carpet repair kit is also included.

Ask for: "Carpets, Cleaning and Repair" (X148A)
Send: $1.00
To: Popular Mechanics
Dept. MP
P.O. Box 1014, Radio City Sta.
New York, NY 10101

MAINTENANCE
To give your carpet the long life it deserves, once-a-week vacuuming is generally a must. If your carpet becomes stained, consult the care manual received at time of purchase, contact your carpet dealer or write to the manufacturer for information on your type of carpeting.

Chemicals

An 8-page booklet describing how to safely use and store household products that contain chemicals, many of them potentially harmful. Written in a question-and-answer format, the booklet tells how to make your home safer, especially if you have children – but even if you don't. It includes a home-safety quiz and an address to write for more information.

Ask for: "The Chemical Do's and Don'ts Book #20"
Send: a postcard
To: Shell Oil Co.
P.O. Box 61609
Houston, TX 77208

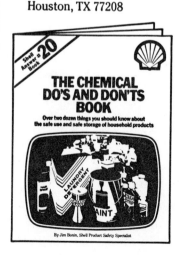

Shell Answer Book 20

THE CHEMICAL DO'S AND DON'TS BOOK

Over two dozen things you should know about the safe use and safe storage of household products

By Jim Bonin, Shell Product Safety Specialist

Home Laundry

A 192-page book called the "Encyclopedia of Home Laundry." This useful book is an alphabetical listing of fabrics, fabric finishes, organizations, chemicals, laundry products and many other items related to the home laundry. A history of laundry and black-and-white illustrations add to the book's considerable value and charm.

Ask for: "Maytag Encyclopedia of Home Laundry"
Send: 50¢
To: Information Ctr.
The Maytag Co.
Newton, IA 50208

Stain Removal

Two liquid-resistant cards with directions for removng spots and stains from carpeting and upholstery. Nearly 50 problem stains are included in these guides. Four cleaning methods will generally remove most household spots and stains.

Ask for: "Bissell Guide to Carpet Spot and Stain Removal" and "Bissell Guide to Upholstery Spot and Stain Removal"
Send: a postcard
To: Betty L. Tisher
Bissell, Inc.
P.O. Box 1888FS
Grand Rapids, MI 49501

Stain Dial

A guide for removing stains. Cut down on expensive dry-cleaning bills by using the "stain dial" tips in your home. An easy-to-use guide, the stain dial provides the right information for removing 56 different types of spots and stains from dry-cleanable fabrics.

Ask for: "K2r® Stain Dial"
Send: a postcard
To: Texize
Consumer Relations Dept., Box MP
P.O. Box 368
Greenville, SC 29602

GUM & GLUE
On carpeting: remove as much of the gum as possible by scraping; "freeze" the residue with ice cubes in a plastic bag. Scrape off brittle gum. Shampoo, let dry and vacuum. For model glue: after removing excess, carefully apply nail polish remover by drops to soften glue. Scrape away. Shampoo, let dry and vacuum.

Appliance Test

A 20-page pamphlet of tips for locating trouble in electrical appliances. Instructions on using a continuity tester are included here, and the various common problems, such as defective cords, faulty switches, stuck thermostat, an open heating element and others, are listed.

Ask for: "Tips on How to Look for Trouble in Electrical Appliances"
Send: a 9″ self-addressed, stamped envelope
To: C.M. Mikolajczyk
Bright Star Industries
Dept. C
600 Getty Ave.
Clifton, NJ 07015

DEFECTIVE CORD

Always suspect a cord that looks frayed or worn. From inside the appliance, disconnect at least one of the appliance cord wires. Short the plug prongs together; then test the cord from inside the appliance with the continuity tester. If the cord has an "open," the flashlight will fail to light.

Burglar Alarms

A 15-page catalog of electronic security equipment and supplies. The catalog offers telephone dialing equipment, ultrasonic motion detectors, burglar alarms, smoke detectors, timers, tear gas and more. Black-and-white photographs, descriptions and prices are provided for each item. An order form and a catalog index are also included.

Ask for: "Sasco Electronic Security Equipment"
Send: a postcard
To: Sasco Burglar Alarms
5619 St. John Ave.
Kansas City, MO 64123

SASCO

ELECTRONIC SECURITY Equipment

AND SUPPLIES

Home Security

An 8-page booklet about easy and inexpensive ways to help protect your home from intruders. It suggests securing windows and doors (including garage doors) and trimming foliage from windows. It also covers the kinds of locks to buy, what to do if you see a burglary in progress, suspicious signs to watch for in your neighborhood and the proper steps to take before leaving on a vacation.

Ask for: "The Home Security Book #16"
Send: a postcard
To: Shell Oil Co.
P.O. Box 61609
Houston, TX 77208

PROTECTION
- Keep a loud noisemaker at home: a police whistle, horn, or, best of all, a barking dog.
- Don't tell a caller that you are home alone.
- Don't publicize your vacations or social events that will take you away from home. Burglars have been known to watch obituaries and steal from the bereaved while they are at the funeral!

GARDEN

Outdoor Gardening

Outdoor Gardening

Seed & Bulbs

Seasonal catalogs for seeds (Jan.-Mar.), bulbs (Mar.-May), harvest (May-July) and fall garden (July-Oct.). These catalogs contain seeds, plants, bulbs and everything for the garden. Kitchen and harvest aids are included in the fall catalog.

Ask for: specific catalog(s) desired
Send: a postcard (one for each catalog requested)
To: your nearest branch of
W. Atlee Burpee Co.
Warminster, PA 18974
(or) Clinton, IA 52732
(or) Riverside, CA 92502

Seeds

An extensive and colorful seed catalog from one of the largest mail-order seed companies in the country. The catalog lists a wide range of flowers, shrubs, trees, fruits and vegetables, including many especially bred for northern climates. Each plant is shown, with specific cultivation tips.

Ask for: "Jung Quality Seeds"
Send: a postcard
To: J.W. Jung Seed Co.
P.O. Box 181
Randolph, WI 53956

Assorted Seeds

An illustrated catalog of seeds for fruits, vegetables and flowers. General instructions for each type of seed are offered, followed by more detailed descriptions for individual varieties. The general instructions include planting times, methods and productivity. Entries for individual varieties describe size, flavor and uses. An order form and ordering instructions are enclosed.

Ask for: "Burrell's Better Seeds Catalog"
Send: a postcard
To: D.V. Burrell Seed Growers Co.
P.O. Box 150H
Rocky Ford, CO 81067

Seeds

An extensive catalog of flower, fruit and vegetable seeds, covering both the familiar and exotic. Has literally hundreds of entries, each with planting and yield information. Other items include shade and nut trees, flowering shrubs, herbs and gardeners' supplies.

Ask for: "Catalog and Planting Guide"
Send: a postcard
To: Earl May Seed and Nursery Co.
80 North Elm
Shenandoah, IA 51603

Seed Packet

A seed packet of your favorite vegetable. Your own homegrown vegetables are tastier and more nutritious than any you can buy, and digging in the garden is great recreation and very satisfying. The packet contains enough seed to produce about 20 feet of the vegetable if a direct sowing method is used.

Ask for: "Seed Packet" (specify type of vegetable seed)
Send: 25¢
To: Butterbrooke Farm
Seed Dept.
78 Barry Rd.
Oxford, CT 06483

Grow Your Own

A full-color catalog of fruit, vegetable and flower seeds. Culture instructions for each type of plant and specific descriptions of individual varieties are included. Herbs, lawn seed and gardening aids are also available.

Ask for: "Wyatt-Quarles Seed Catalog"
Send: a postcard
To: Wyatt-Quarles Seed Co.
Dept. MBP
P.O. Box 2131
Raleigh, NC 27602

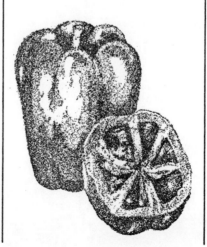

Outdoor Gardening

Seeds & Supplies

An indexed catalog of plants, seeds and supplies for the garden, nursery and greenhouse. Bushes and trees for the yard, as well as fruits, flowers and vegetables, are included. An order form and instructions are provided.

Ask for: "Mellinger's Plant, Seed and Supply Catalog"
Send: a postcard
To: Mellinger's Inc.
2310 W. South Range Rd.
North Lima, OH 44452

Seeds & Care

A catalog of vegetable and flower seeds and a 23-page pamphlet of tips on growing bedding plants. The catalog includes price lists and an order form for a large variety of seeds, plus a section with a booklist to aid the gardener. The planning, preparation and care of bedding plants are explained in the pamphlet.

Ask for: "Garden Catalog" and "Bedding Plant Handbook"
Send: $1.00
To: Bonavista
Dept. 200
P.O. Box 813
Laramie, WY 82070

Flowers & Vegetables

An illustrated catalog of vegetables and flower seeds with "aids to good growing." Descriptions include length, size and color of the various species, as well as some planting information. The catalog is indexed, and an order form is enclosed.

Ask for: "Harris Vegetable & Flower Seeds"
Send: a postcard
To: Harris Seeds
5 Moreton Farm
Rochester, NY 14624

GARDEN SOIL
Prepare a good garden soil by mixing about 2" of organic matter (such as peat moss or leafmold) to your present soil. Add 1 to 2 lbs. of 10-10-10 (10% nitrogen, 10% phosphorus, 10% potash) or 12-12-12 (12% nitrogen, 12% phosphorus, 12% potash) fertilizer per 100 sq. ft. before planting. Water vegetable bedding plants thoroughly when you plant.

Plants

A large seed catalog of useful plants, including vegetables, flowers, fruits, nuts, herbs, dye plants and more. The catalog provides growing instructions for all seeds and the history and nutritional values of some vegetables. Drawings of more unusual plants are included, as well as a large selection of books.

Ask for: "Catalog of Useful Plants"
Send: 50¢ (in stamps or coin)
To: Craig Dremann, Prop.
Redwood City Seed Co.
P.O. Box 361
Redwood City, CA 94064

Complete Seeds

An extensive catalog of all kinds of seeds – flowers, decorative plants and shrubs, vegetables, herbs, cacti and special Mexican plants. They are listed alphabetically by Latin name and indexed by common name. Some illustrations are included, as well as plant descriptions and germination instructions. Complete ordering instructions and order form.

Ask for: "The Complete Catalog of Seeds"
Send: $1.00
To: J.L. Hudson's World Seed Service
P.O. Box 1058FS
Redwood City, CA 94064

Seeds & Supplies

A 72-page catalog of flower and vegetable seeds and gardening supplies. Descriptions of the adult plants and planting information are provided. Planting charts for vegetables are included, as is a chart that details the percentage of U.S. recommended daily allowances for vitamins, minerals and proteins provided by vegetables and fruits.

Ask for: "Herbst Brothers Seedsmen Catalog"
Send: a postcard
To: Herbst Brothers Seedsmen, Inc.
1000-F Main St.
Brewster, NY 10509

Outdoor Gardening

Small Gardens

A catalog of flower and vegetable seeds for people with small gardens. The catalog offers small seed packets at reduced prices so that gardeners with limited space can afford to experiment with many different varieties. About 220 varieties are described, along with growing time and price per packet. The catalog includes a guarantee and an order form.

Ask for: "Seed Catalog"
Send: a postcard
To: Pine Tree Seed Co.
Dept. FS
P.O. Box 1399
Portland, ME 04104

Garden Seeds

A catalog filled with vegetable and flower seeds, including many that are especially adapted to northern climates. The catalog contains detailed descriptions of plants and vegetables, culture information, photographs and directions for storing many vegetables. Some gardening and greenhouse supplies are offered.

Ask for: "Free Seed Catalog"
Send: a postcard
To: Stokes Seeds, Inc.
P.O. Box 548
737 Main St.
Buffalo, NY 14240

Vegetables

A large catalog of vegetable seeds especially for gardeners in northern regions and those interested in organic growing. The catalog lists over 500 types of vegetable seeds, including some herb and farm seeds, along with exhaustive growing instructions and notes on diseases and pests. Also lists select equipment, gardening books and useful planting information.

Ask for: "Johnny's Selected Seeds"
Send: a postcard
To: Johnny's Selected Seeds
Albion, ME 04910

Southern Gardens

An extensive catalog, issued twice yearly, that specializes in seed and nursery stock especially well adapted to the South. Vegetables, flowers, nuts and berries can be found in this nicely detailed, colorfully illustrated catalog. An order form is included.

Ask for: "Hastings Garden Catalog"
Send: a postcard
To: H.G. Hastings Co.
Dept. MP
P.O. Box 4274
Atlanta, GA 30302

Florida Seeds

A catalog of vegetable and flower seeds, many treated to resist insects and diseases. The catalog includes some color and many black-and-white photographs, along with plant descriptions, growing instructions and seed prices per packet, ounce, 1/4-pound and pound. Special features are sections on planting by the stars and on common garden insects, with photographs and notes on how to control them.

Ask for: "Kilgore Seed Catalog and Planting Guide"
Send: 50¢
To: Kilgore Seed Co.
1400 W. First St. — MP
Sanford, FL 32771

Roses

A catalog of miniature roses. The catalog offers many varieties of miniatures, including miniature tree roses, climbing varieties, hanging-basket varieties and moss roses. Color photographs of several roses complement their written descriptions. An inserted card provides growing instructions, and an order blank is included.

Ask for: "Catalog of Miniature Roses"
Send: a postcard
To: Sequoia Nursery
Moore Miniature Roses
2519 E. Noble Ave.
Visalia, CA 93277

Outdoor Gardening

Wildflowers

A large, beautifully photographed foldout picturing 29 species of wildflowers, sent along with a sample packet of seeds. Includes information on such flowers as the California Poppy, Blue Lupine, Golden-Eyed Grass, Coast Trillium and Mule's Ear Daisy.

Ask for: wildflower brochure and sample seed packet
Send: 35¢ and a 9″ self-addressed, stamped envelope
To: Clyde Robin Seed Co., Inc.
  P.O. Box 2855MP
  Castro Valley, CA 94546

Wildflowers & Ferns

A price list of wildflowers and ferns. Each entry includes planting and culture information, along with a general description of the plant. Examples of stock are Showy Ladyslipper, Bloodroot, Blue Flag Iris, Anemone, Marsh Marigold, Clintonia, Cypripediums, Shooting Star, Trout Lily, Wild Geranium, Hepatica Triloba, Virginia Blue Bell and Birdfoot Violet.

Ask for: wildflower price list
Send: a 9″ self-addressed, stamped envelope
To: Ferndale Nursery
  P.O. Box 218
  Askov, MN 55704

Ferndale Nursery and Greenhouse
P. O. Box 218
ASKOV, MINNESOTA 55704

Blue Ridge Wildflowers

A 40-page catalog of wildflowers from the Blue Ridge Mountains. The varieties include perennials, rock garden plants, orchids, ferns, bog plants, vines, climbers, creepers, lilies, deciduous trees and shrubs, and evergreen trees and shrubs. Photographs of some of the available plants highlight the catalog.

Ask for: "Gardens of the Blue Ridge Catalog"
Send: a postcard
To: Gardens of the Blue Ridge
  Edw. P. Robbins
  P.O. Box 10
  Pineola, NC 28662

PLANTING

For all perennials, rock garden plants, ferns, bog plants, hardy vines, climbers, creepers and ground covers: growing crowns, buds or roots should be placed 1 to 2 inches below the surface, according to size. Soil should be firm about the roots and smooth on the surface. Mulch with leaves or litter in the late fall, allowing this to remain through the winter. Remove the mulch in early spring.

Fruit

A colorful booklet picturing and describing dozens of fruit-bearing plants. Offers many varieties of strawberries and raspberries, plus apple, peach, pear, cherry and apricot trees. Also includes decorative trees and shrubs. Gives specific information on the plants' characteristics. As a bonus, you can send for a hanging strawberry plant.

Ask for: catalog **and/or** hanging strawberry plant
Send: postcard for catalog **and/or** 50¢ for hanging strawberry plant
To: Dean Foster Nurseries
Box FSG
Rte. 2
Hartford, MI 49057

Orchard Trees

A large catalog featuring everything for the home orchard – dwarf, semi-dwarf and standard apples, peaches, nectarines, pears, cherries, apricots and plums. The catalog also offers ornamental trees, nut trees, roses and berries. Pollination information and growing tips are included, along with color photographs of the fruit.

Ask for: "Fruit Tree & Garden Catalog"
Send: a postcard
To: Stark Bro.'s Nurseries
P.O. Box A299CO
Louisiana, MO 63353

JERSEYMAC
This smooth, red-skinned, McIntosh-type apple is vigorous and easy to grow, succeeding in hot summer areas where regular McIntosh has difficulty. Its slightly tart flavor makes for good fresh eating and excellent sauces and pies. Recommended pollinators are McIntosh and Starkspur Golden Delicious.

Fruit Gardens

An 8-page price and variety list of fruits. Those included are apples, pears, peaches, nectarines, plums, apricots, cherries, quinces, currants, gooseberries, grapes and conservation fruits. Ordering information is included.

Ask for: "Southmeadow Fruit Gardens Price and Variety List"
Send: a postcard
To: Southmeadow Fruit Gardens
2363 Tilbury Pl.
Birmingham, MI 48009

Southmeadow Fruit Gardens

Outdoor Gardening

Garlic

A specialty catalog of garlics for planting or eating. The catalog offers elephant garlic, Italian garlic, German red garlic, shallots, Egyptian onions, comfrey and horseradish roots. The catalog includes background information on the company and on the garlics, helpful serving suggestions and an order blank.

Ask for: catalog
Send: a postcard
To: S & H Organic Acres
  P.O. Box 27M
  Montgomery Creek, CA 96065

Oriental Seeds

A catalog featuring Chinese vegetable seeds, cookware and seasonings **and/or** a packet of one of the following vegetable seeds: Chinese white cabbage, snow peas, Chinese parsley, Chinese kale, asparagus bean, Chinese winter melon, Chinese okra, chinese chives and India mustard.

Ask for: "Free Catalog" **and/or** "Catalog and Seed packet" (specify type of seed)
Send: a postcard for catalog alone; 85¢ for the catalog and seed packet
To: Tsang and Ma Intl.
  1306F Old County Rd.
  Belmont, CA 94002

Mexican Tomatoes

A packet of 85 seeds plus organic growing instructions. These seeds produce delicious, giant tomatoes which can exceed 3 pounds. They are thick-meated with few seeds and are vigorous productive growers.

Ask for: "Holmes Mexican Tomato"
Send: $1.00
To: M.P. Quisenberry
  4626 Glebe Farm Rd.
  Sarasota, FL 33580

Herb Seeds

A packet of herb seeds (chosen from a wide selection in stock). The packet itself describes the herb by its common name, Latin name and family, height and the type of soil and light it needs. Instructions on sowing, thinning and harvesting are included, as are suggested uses.

Ask for: "Helix Herb Seeds"
Send: a 9″ self-addressed, stamped envelope
To: Helix Corp.
  Dept. AL
  4770 Pearl St.
  Boulder, CO 80301

Seed Packets

Six herb seed packets to start your own herb garden. The packets include dill, sweet fennel, curled cress, coriander, fenugreek and luffa (also known as dishcloth gourd).

Ask for: "Herb Seed Packets"
Send: $1.00
To: Yankee Peddler Herb Farm
  Dept. MBP
  Rte. 1, Box 251A
  Burton, TX 77835

Herb Almanac

A 64-page almanac/catalog packed with information about herbs and herbal products. This almanac includes astronomical information, monthly planting guides, weather forecasts and historic events. A variety of seeds, beans, herbs, oils and related products, as well as books on these topics, are available. An order form and instructions are included.

Ask for: "The Herbalist Almanac"
Send: 95¢
To: Indiana Botanic Gardens, Inc.
  P.O. Box 5FS
  Hammond, IN 46325

HERB USES
Fenugreek has a maple-like flavor and is used for baked goods, syrups and candies. It is also sprouted and used in salads. The luffa is dried and used as a sponge, or cooked (when young) and eaten like summer squash. The dill, sweet fennel, curled cress and coriander are used in salads and as seasoning.

Outdoor Gardening

Vegetable Gardening

A 144-page guide to "growing your own vegetables." This comprehensive booklet offers a series of short essays on all aspects of vegetable gardening. Planning, growing transplants, planting and other topics on the subject of growing vegetables are included.

Ask for: "Growing Your Own Vegetables" (AB409)
Send: a postcard
To: Publications Div.
Office of Governmental and Public Affairs
U.S. Dept. of Agriculture
Washington, DC 20250

Growing Your Own Vegetables

Garden Hints

A 32-page tabloid filled with gardening information. From planning to harvesting, nearly everything you need to know about gardening is available here. Planting guides, mulching, insect identification and control, and detailed information about a wide range of vegetables are among the topics discussed.

Ask for: "The Garden Tabloid" (Pub. 1091)
Send: a postcard
To: Ms. Nancy B. Sweet, Editor
P.O. Box 5404MSU
Mississippi Coop. Extension Service
Mississippi State, MS 39762

PLAN FIRST
The first step toward a successful garden is the complete planning. This involves selecting the site, choosing the vegetables and choosing the amount of each kind. Draw a plan on paper, showing the location of each vegetable, the expected planting date, the length of row for each and what is to follow when you harvest each crop.

Vegetables

A 64-page booklet on basic vegetable gardening. Nearly all you need to know about vegetable gardening is well presented in this attractive, illustrated booklet from Northrup King. From the reasons why gardening is growing in popularity to suggestions about planting, this guide offers much valuable information to home gardeners.

Ask for: "Basic Vegetable Gardening Guide"
Send: $1.00
To: Guide
One Industrial Dr.
P.O. Box 2966
Maple Plain, MN 55348

NORTHRUP KING'S
Basic Vegetable Gardening Guide

How to raise and prepare vegetables with that mulchless homegrown taste

Home Gardens

An extensive, 31-page booklet giving an overview of the considerations faced by the home vegetable gardener. Explores location, soils, equipment, fertilization, crop choice, seeds vs. plants, planting, marking and spacing rows, thinning, transplanting, hot-caps, irrigation, weed control, mulches, disease and pest control.

Ask for: "The Home Vegetable Garden" (IB101)
Send: 75¢
To: Distribution Ctr.—F
7 Research Park
Cornell University
Ithaca, NY 14850

Seed Producing

A 6-page booklet about growing vegetables for seed. Meant especially for gardeners in areas of the U.S. with warm winters, the booklet explains how to collect seeds from the most common vegetable crops. The booklet includes a list of materials needed as well as instructions for each type of vegetable.

Ask for: "Vegetable Seed Production in the S.F. Bay Area of California and Other Warm-Winter Areas of the U.S."
Send: 50¢ (stamps or coins)
To: Craig Dremann, Prop.
Redwood City Seed Co.
P.O. Box 361
Redwood City, CA 94064

Tomatoes

A 14-page, illustrated booklet on growing tomatoes. The topics include choosing suitable tomato varieties, selecting a site, preparing the soil, seeding, care, harvest and pest control. Black-and-white photographs show the tomato at each stage of development, from seed to mature plant.

Ask for: "Growing Tomatoes in the Home Garden"
Send: $1.00
To: Consumer Information Ctr.
Dept. 177H
Pueblo, CO 81009

ASPARAGUS
Sow seed or plant roots in rich soil in the spring. In the second year, berries form. Harvest when they turn red and before frost. Crush and put in water. Pulp will float to the top and seeds will sink. Dry seeds immediately by spreading thin on screens in the sun. Dry 2-3 weeks before storing. Storage life: 3 years.

Outdoor Gardening

Assorted Berries

A large, 5-page foldout giving information on successful culture of blackberries, currants and gooseberries. Outlines varieties of each species, selection of location and soil, propagation, culture, pruning, insects, diseases and procedures to avoid. Includes photo illustrations.

Ask for: "Blackberries, Currants and Gooseberries" (IB97)
Send: 30¢
To: Distribution Ctr. – F
7 Research Park
Cornell University
Ithaca, NY 14850

BLACKBERRY LOCATION
A fertile, sandy loam soil, high in organic matter, is preferred. A slight slope with good water drainage all year and no frost pockets will contribute to success. Avoid proximity to wild or older raspberries and blackberries, light droughty or heavy clay soils, and areas infested with perennial weeds.

Fruits & Nuts

A 52-page, illustrated booklet on "Growing Fruits and Nuts." All possible considerations in the home cultivation of fruits and nuts, from selection to planting to pest control, are taken into account in this informative collection of brief essays.

Ask for: "Growing Fruits and Nuts" (AB408)
Send: a postcard
To: Publications Div.
Office of Governmental and Public Affairs
U.S. Dept. of Agriculture
Washington, DC 20250

Growing
Fruits and Nuts

Growing Peaches

A detailed, illustrated, 16-page booklet conveying information on methods for successful peach growing. Covers choosing a location for the orchard, planting, stock selection, land preparation, spacing, erosion control, pruning, cover crops, mulch, herbicides, fertilizers, thinning, pollination and harvesting.

Ask for: "Peach Growing" (IB44)
Send: 75¢
To: Distribution Ctr.–F
7 Research Park
Cornell University
Ithaca, NY 14850

PICKING
When the peaches have reached the desired stage of maturity, the fruit should be picked by taking it gently in the palm of the hand and twisting it sideways to prevent bruising and tearing of the flesh around the stem. Removal with the fingertips is likely to result in bruising and discoloration.

Dwarf Trees

An 8-page, illustrated booklet on the selection and care of dwarf fruit trees. The types of dwarf fruit trees available and their sizes are discussed, along with the importance of soil, early fruit production and pruning. Proper care – including training, fertilizing, mulching and pest control – is also reviewed.

Ask for: "Dwarf Fruit Trees"
Send: $1.00
To: Consumer Information Ctr.
Dept. 195H
Pueblo, CO 81009

Dwarf Fruit Trees
Selection and Care

Grafting

An extensive, illustrated, 7-page booklet giving instruction in top-working and bridge-grafting fruit trees. Outlines the essentials of grafting, seasonal considerations, selection and storage of scion wood, protection of the graft, whip-grafting and budding. Drawings detail specifics of procedures.

Ask for: "Top-Working and Bridge-Grafting Fruit Trees" (IB75)
Send: 35¢
To: Distribution Ctr. – F
7 Research Park
Cornell University
Ithaca, NY 14850

Top-Working and Bridge-Grafting Fruit Trees

Flowers

A detailed, illustrated booklet giving tips on growing flowers from seed. Topics include both indoor and outdoor sowing; use of cold frames and hotbeds; transplanting; use of fluorescent lights, sphagnum moss and vermiculite; and seed stratification. Lists optimum planting times, annuals that often self-sow, perennials that are difficult to grow in this manner.

Ask for: "Flowers from Seed" (IB20)
Send: 35¢
To: Distribution Ctr. – F
7 Research Park
Cornell University
Ithaca, NY 14850

USE OF SEED
It is generally advisable to purchase seed from a reliable dealer, since seed produced by natural pollination may not produce plants typical of the parents. This is especially true of hybrids, such as petunias, oriental poppies, perennial phlox and the like.

Outdoor Gardening

Perennials

A 32-page, brightly illustrated booklet on the subject of growing flowering perennials. Helpful suggestions are offered on a variety of topics including planning the garden, planting and growing. A section on starting the plants indoors is also provided.

Ask for: "Growing Flowering Perennials"
Send: $1.00
To: Consumer Information Ctr.
    Dept. 128H
    Pueblo, CO 81009

STAKING
You can use stakes made of twigs, wood dowels, bamboo, wire or even plastic. Select stakes that will be 6-12 inches shorter than the height of the plant. Place the stakes behind the plants. Sink the stakes into the ground far enough to be firm. Loosely tie plants to the stakes.

Ornamental Grasses

An illustrated, informative, 15-page booklet detailing selection and use of ornamental grasses in the home garden. Describes 41 ornamental grasses, landscape and climatic considerations, grasses for dried arrangements, culture and maintenance.

Ask for: "Ornamental Grasses for the Home and Garden" (IB64)
Send: 30¢
To: Distribution Ctr. – F
    7 Research Park
    Cornell University
    Ithaca, NY 14850

Ornamental Grasses for the Home and Garden

Shore Gardens

A foldout about the plants most suitable for seashore gardening, particularly along the Connecticut coast. The foldout lists annuals, trees that make good windbreaks and native plants that can be transplanted. The foldout also provides a few tips about shore gardening and the addresses of University of Connecticut county extension offices.

Ask for: "Plants for the Seashore"
Send: 25¢
To: U-35
    College of Agriculture and
      Natural Resources
    Storrs, CT 06268

TIPS
- A key to better seashore gardening is to plant all plants closer together than normal. That way they will aid each other in remaining upright during storms.
- Plants with fine foliage do well as seashore plantings, because less damage occurs from wind blowing at the leaves.

Trees

A 20-page booklet on the use of trees to enhance urban and suburban environments. Describes tree selection, needs of and benefits offered by various types of trees, climatic considerations and the limitations imposed by some soil types. Outlines dozens of species according to size, growth rate, description and where they can thrive.

Ask for: "Trees for a More Livable Environment"
Send: 50¢
To: Educational Materials
Chevron Chemical Co.
Public Affairs Dept.
P.O. Box 3744
San Francisco, CA 94119

Landscaping

A foldout for homeowners with poor growing conditions on their lots, especially for areas where bulldozers have left poor soil to be landscaped. The foldout lists plants that will grow in difficult situations, such as in the shade in well-drained or poorly drained soil, on hot and dry slopes and in heavy clay soil. The foldout also provides some insecticide safety tips.

Ask for: "Plants for Difficult Situations"
Send: 25¢
To: U-35
College of Agriculture and
Natural Resources
Storrs, CT 06268

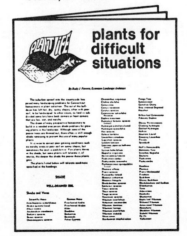

Landscaping

A short foldout on basic landscaping principles. Discusses the 3 areas of your property – the public, private and service areas – but concentrates mainly on landscaping to enhance the front of the house. Contains a number of simple and useful ideas for improving the looks and livability of your property.

Ask for: "Home Beautification"
Send: a 9″ self-addressed, stamped envelope
To: Information Div.
West Virginia Dept. of
Agriculture
Charleston, WV 25305

Outdoor Gardening

Drainage

An informative, illustrated foldout that discusses drainage around your home. Among the topics considered are flooding, springs, seeps, the seasonal high-water table, the ponding of surface water, slow soil permeability and the most effective methods for getting help when a problem occurs.

Ask for: "Drainage Around Your Home"
Send: $1.00
To: Consumer Information Ctr.
   Dept. 156J
   Pueblo, CO 81009

PONDING
If surface water ponds on your lawn or driveway, you can install small diversions or ditches to channel off the water. In developed residental areas, these structures usually are installed near property lines in back of or alongside houses.

Irrigation

Two 8-page booklets about a sub-surface irrigation system that uses up to 80% less water than surface systems and requires no electricity or maintenance. The booklets explain the advantages of this system for use in agriculture, orchards and private residences.

Ask for: "The Irrigation Solution for 80% Water and Energy Savings" and "The Irrigation Solution: Waterguarde Automated Sub-Surface Irrigation Control"
Send: a postcard
To: Waterguarde
   Automated Sub-Surface
   Irrigation
   P.O. Box 1222
   La Mesa, CA 92041

The Irrigation Solution

For 80% Water and Energy Savings

It's the most advanced irrigation system yet developed. Because it's so simple.

It needs virtually no maintenance. It eliminates weeds and erosion. It gives only as much water as needed — no waste. Installation is easy. And it provides years and years of dependable service.

It's called Waterguarde.

Irrigation

An 8-page booklet and a catalog about a drip-irrigation system. The illustrated, full-color booklet explains the advantages of drip irrigation. The booklet and catalog offer system components and provide instructions to help readers plan, design and install an irrigation system suited to their needs.

Ask for: "Submatic Irrigation Systems" and "Submatic Drip-Irrigation Catalog"
Send: a postcard
To: Submatic
   Dept. GF
   P.O. Box 246
   Lubbock, TX 79408

EMITTER
A drip-irrigation system is relatively simple. The essential item is the emitter, a fitting with a small orifice. When plugged into a flexible type hose, it emits about 1 gallon of water per hour. Emitters are usually spaced about every 2 feet in the house, and then the hose is laid by each row of plants.

Vegetable Diseases

An informative, illustrated, 18-page booklet on insects and diseases in the home vegetable garden. Outlines types of insects and causes of diseases, along with methods of control. Describes chemical, biological and botanical insecticides; fungicides; seed treatments; application methods and safety in use; handling and storage of chemicals.

Ask for: "Insects and Diseases in the Home Vegetable Garden" (IB141)
Send: $1.00
To: Distribution Ctr. – F
7 Research Park
Cornell University
Ithaca, NY 14850

Insects and Diseases in the Home Vegetable Garden

(booklet cover reproduced with illustrative body text)

Plant Diseases

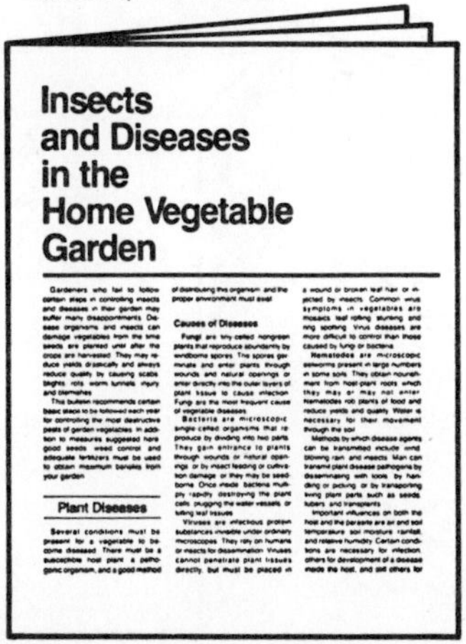

Fruit Diseases

An information-packed, illustrated, 16-page booklet on diseases and insects affecting home orchards. Details types of insects and causes of disease, together with methods of control. Covers such diseases as apple scab, mildew, rot and canker; also discusses insects such as aphids, mites, maggots and borers.

Ask for: "Disease and Insect Control in the Home Orchard" (IB124)
Send: $1.00
To: Distribution Ctr. – F
7 Research Park
Cornell University
Ithaca, NY 14850

CONTROL

It is helpful in disease control to prune out dead twigs and branches while the trees are dormant. Destroy diseased fruit and leaves somewhere away from fruit trees and follow a regular spray program tailored to the fruit crops you are growing.

Weeds

A 16-page booklet providing information on the weeds that most often plague the home gardener. Pictured and described are amaranth pigweed, burdock, chickweed, chicory, common mallow, curly dock, dandelion, field buttercup, lamb's quarters, wild mustard, yellow rocket, crabgrass, green foxtail, milkweed, ragweed and others.

Ask for: "Weeds" (IB72)
Send: 25¢
To: Distribution Ctr. – F
7 Research Park
Cornell University
Ithaca, NY 14850

Weeds

Outdoor Gardening

Lawn Insects

A 20-page illustrated booklet on insect control. Pests that infest soil and roots, feed on leaves and stems, suck plant juice and inhabit but do not damage lawns are discussed, with suggestions for appropriate measures for their control. The booklet also outlines special precautions in using pesticides.

Ask for: "Lawn Insects: How to Control Them"
Send: $1.00
To: Consumer Information Ctr.
Dept. 198H
Pueblo, CO 81009

LAWN INSECTS: How to Control Them

Pest Control

A foldout and several information sheets on the use of ladybugs and the Chinese praying mantis for control of insect pests, as opposed to use of insecticide chemicals. Included are tips on successful storage and application, along with description of the characteristics of ladybugs and mantises and how they work in the garden.

Ask for: "Biological Control Information"
Send: a postcard
To: Bio-Control Co.
P.O. Box 247
13451 Hwy. 174
Cedar Ridge, CA 95924

LADYBIRD BEETLES
Ladybird beetles live approximately 1 year and can eat as many as 40-50 aphids per day. They also destroy fruit scales, mealybugs, bollworms, leafworms, leafhoppers, fleahoppers and corn-ear worms. They do not eat vegetation.

Pest Control

A foldout/catalog of natural pesticides. Among those available are a general purpose insecticide, as well as controls for caterpillars, mites, fungus, ants and roaches. A chart is provided to give additional information about which products are useful for specific types of pests.

Ask for: "Nature's Own Powerful Pesticides"
Send: a postcard
To: Organic Control, Inc.
P.O. Box 25382CX
Los Angeles, CA 90025

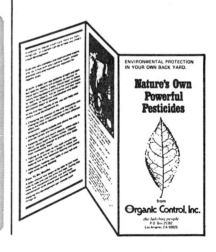

Insect Control

A brief foldout on biological insect control. The Trichogramma wasp is harmless to everything except the undesirable Lepidopterous eggs; this foldout carefully explains why and how the wasp should be used to control insect pests. Information on ordering "Trik-O" eggs is included.

Ask for: "Trichogramma Brochure"
Send: a postcard
To: Gothard, Inc.
Dept. FS
P.O. Box 370
Canutillo, TX 79835

Pesticides

A foldout reference guide on the subject of pesticides for home gardeners. The guide covers diseases and descriptions of injury of trees, vegetables, lawns and flowers. A number of different pesticides and their common uses are listed in this guide.

Ask for: "Bonide Home Gardeners' Pesticide Reference Guide"
Send: a 9″ self-addressed, stamped envelope
To: Bonide Chemical Co., Inc.
2 Wurz Ave.
Yorkville, NY 13495

Chemical Safety

A colorful, concise foldout outlining safety considerations related to garden chemicals. Correct procedures for mixing and applying, storage, disposal and first aid are explained, along with how to handle spills. May be used as a poster in garage or shed for quick, convenient reference.

Ask for: "Garden Chemicals and Common Sense"
Send: a postcard
To: Consumer Products
Chevron Chemical Co.
P.O. Box 7335
San Francisco, CA 94105

EXAMPLES
A partial list of insects controlled by the use of Trichogramma includes codling moths in fruit, army worms, European corn borers, cotton bollworms, leaf rollers, pecan casebearers, tomato fruitworms, some cutworms, corn earworms and spring cankerworms (inchworms).

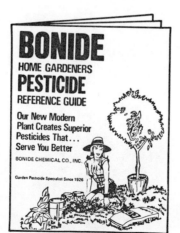

READ THE LABEL
It's a must if you want to know if you're using the right product for the job, know the right protective measures and know what to do before an accident occurs. Also, the label will tell you how to dispose of container and any unused product so as to protect family, friends, pets and wildlife.

Outdoor Gardening

Garden News

A sample copy of *Gardens for All News.* This magazine includes how-to-garden information for new and experienced vegetable gardeners, plus stories about how people around the country use garden projects to offset inflation and improve community life.

Ask for: a sample copy of *Gardens for All News*
Send: a postcard
To: David Schaefer
Gardens for All
180 Flynn Ave., Dept. FS
Burlington, VT 05401

GIANT FRUITS
Here's a trick for growing gargantuan fruits: Select a promising baby peach, pear, plum or apple, and insert it (still on its branch) in a large glass bottle. Prop up the bottle to support the branch, and watch it grow in its warm, humid "mini-greenhouse."

Growing Tips

A sample copy of the latest issue of *The Family Food Garden,* a magazine containing tips and detailed information on growing food crops. Recent articles have dealt with production hints, harvesting blueberries in 2 years, making pickles and growing everything from saffron to cauliflower. Plus tips on making jams, aromatic blends and a portable potting station.

Ask for: a sample copy of *The Family Food Garden*
Send: $1.00
To: The Family Food Garden
Reader Services, Dept. MP
1999 Shepard Rd.
St. Paul, MN 55116

Gourds

A sample of *The Gourd* magazine, plus 2 short information sheets, one on "Gourds: Their Culture and Use" and another entitled "So Your Gourds Rotted: Or Did They?" The magazine, published 3 times yearly, contains articles, letters, descriptions of books and bulletins of interest.

Ask for: *The Gourd,* "Gourds: Their Culture and Use" and "So Your Gourds Rotted: Or Did They?"
Send: 50¢ **and** a 9″ self-addressed, stamped envelope
To: American Gourd Soc.
P.O. Box 274M
Mt. Gilead, OH 43338

Horticultural News

A sample copy of the *Avant Gardener,* a newsletter chronicling developments in the horticultural field. Published semi-monthly, this publication includes short articles and news briefs on the wide range of topics encountered by the gardener.

Ask for: a sample copy of *The Avant Gardener*
Send: $1.00
To: The Avant Gardener
P.O. Box 489
New York, NY 10028

Lawn Care

A 2-year subscription to *Lawn Care,* a mini-magazine to aid homeowners who would like to have a satisfying lawn wherever they live. The magazine includes short feature articles; advice on fertilization, seeding and weed control; a question-and-answer section; and a garden supplement.

Ask for: a subscription to *Lawn Care*
Send: a postcard
To: Scott's Lawn Care Subscriptions
Marysville, OH 43041

Resources

A 47-page pamphlet listing available informational and instructional materials on a wide variety of subjects. Topics include home gardening, food crops, bees, food preservation, fruits and nuts, herbs, organic gardening and composting, pest control, flowers, houseplants, lawns and landscaping, ornamentals, poisonous plants and tree and wildlife identification.

Ask for: "The Know How Catalog"
Send: a postcard
To: Distribution Ctr.—F
7 Research Park
Cornell University
Ithaca, NY 14850

GERMINATION
For very fast germination of seeds, soak them in a solution of 3 teaspoons Basic-H to 1 gallon of water. Sprout seeds in egg cartons, putting seed and a small amount of solution in each cup.

LAWN DISEASE
To virtually assure freedom from disease problems, supplement normal good lawn practices by applying a disease-preventer product. Choose one that is effective against a wide spectrum of fungi. Use it in fall and again in spring.

Outdoor Gardening

Government Catalogs

Two catalogs from the U.S. Government Printing Office listing many pamphlets and booklets on gardening that readers can purchase through the mail.

Ask for: "Home Gardening of Fruits and Vegetables" (SB-001) and "Floriculture" (SB-038)
Send: a postcard
To: Superintendent of Documents
U.S. Government Printing Office
Washington, DC 20402

Gardening Books

A comprehensive, 66-page catalog of books on many subjects of interest to the gardener. Sample topics include gardening, greenhouses, composting and insect control. Instructions for ordering are included.

Ask for: "Mother's Bookshelf Catalog"
Send: a postcard
To: Mother's Bookshelf
Dept. FS
P.O. Box 70
Hendersonville, NC 28791

Books & Bulletins

A checklist of books and bulletins of interest to the gardener. The topics include gardening, insect control, composting, small-scale farming and much more. Ordering information is provided.

Ask for: "Country Wisdom Books and Bulletins"
Send: a postcard
To: Garden Way Publishing
Dept. A564
Charlotte, VT 05445

BEST BETS
- "Growing Vegetables in the Home Garden." A step-by-step guide for the would-be gardener.
- "Lawn Insects: How to Control Them." A booklet that describes how insects infest soil and roots and feed on leaves, stems and plant juice.

BEST BETS
- *Fruits and Berries for the Home Garden* (Lewis Hill)
- *Let It Rot! The Home Gardener's Guide to Composting* (Stu Campbell)
- *Growing and Saving Vegetable Seeds* (Marc Rogers)
- *The Bug Book: Harmless Insect Controls* (John and Helen Philbrick)

Books & More

A 34-page catalog of dried herbs, seeds, books, botanicals, teas and plants. Culinary, medicinal and ornamental herbs in plant and seed form are available, as are herb products including teas and body care items. Books available cover such topics as herb knowledge, cookbooks, gardening, medicine and survival.

Ask for: "The Yankee Peddler Catalog"
Send: $1.00
To: Yankee Peddler Herb Farm
Dept. MBP
Rte. 1, Box 251A
Burton, TX 77835

Garden Tools

An illustrated, 32-page catalog of high-quality garden tools. For each tool, the catalog presents drawings, specific uses and specifications such as length, weight and head size. It also provides a description of the manufacturer and of the particular construction processes used in making each tool. Includes a price list and order blank.

Ask for: "Smith & Hawken Tool Company Catalog"
Send: a postcard
To: Smith & Hawken Tool Co.
68 Homer
Drawer 086
Palo Alto, CA 94301

Vegetable Trellis

An information sheet and an actual sample of nylon netting used in a grid configuration as a vegetable trellis. Advantages of nylon netting include the fact that it is weather- and rot-resistant, won't burn or rust plants, and is easily cut to the desired size.

Ask for: vegetable trellis sample
Send: a 9" self-addressed, stamped envelope
To: Fanon Designs, Inc.
700 Langford Dr.
Norcross, GA 30071

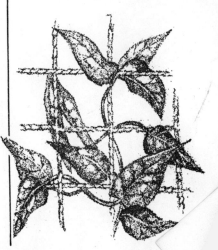

Outdoor Gardening

Canning & Freezing

Four informative publications that provide instructions for canning and freezing everything from fruits and vegetables to meats.

- **"10 Short Lessons in Canning & Freezing"**
- **"Kerr Home Canning & Freezing Guide"**
- **"The Fact Sheet"**
- **"Pickle Pointers"**

Ask for: each publication you want by name
Send: a postcard
To: Home Economist, JGB
    Consumer Products Div.
    Kerr Glass Mfg. Corp.
    Sand Springs, OK 74063

Home Canning

A foldout that explains the 3 different methods for home canning — open kettle, boiling water bath and pressure canning. Charts give the number of minutes each type of food should be boiled. The foldout gives numerous tips on canning techniques and also includes information on botulism.

Ask for: "Successful Home Canning"
Send: a 9" self-addressed, stamped envelope
To: Information Div.
    West Virginia Dept. of
    Agriculture
    Charleston, WV 25305

PRESERVATION
Food is canned or processed to preserve it for later use. The principle behind the canning process is to heat the food hot enough to render harmless the various molds, yeasts and bacteria that cause food spoilage and to seal the food in airtight containers so such organisms cannot get in.

Home Canning

An illustrated, 16-page tabloid on home canning. The information presented includes the necessary materials, a chart on how to figure the yield of canned fruits and vegetables from fresh, pickling advice and recipes, directions for fruit and vegetable canning, and recipes for jelly, jam and preserves.

Ask for: "Home Canning Tabloid" (Pub. 1152)
Send: a postcard
To: Ms. Nancy B. Sweet, Pub. Editor
    P.O. Box 5404MSU
    Mississippi Coop. Extension
    Service
    Mississippi State, MS 39762

SPOILAGE
Always be on the lookout for any signs of spoilage. Never use any food that is questionable. Look closely at each container before using it. Bulging lids or rings, or a leak, may mean that the seal has broken and the food has spoiled. When you open a container, look for other signs — spurting liquid, an odor or mold.

Food Processing

A 24-page catalog of food and food-related items for use in the home. Everything from food dehydrators to cookbooks to sprouting supplies are included. Anyone interested in naturally processed foods will find a wide variety of useful tools here. A drawing or photograph illustrates each item.

Ask for: "Family Health and Survival Catalog"
Send: 50¢
To: Great Northern Distributing Co.
325 Pierpont Ave.
Salt Lake City, UT 84101

Storing Produce

An 18-page, illustrated booklet on storing fruits and vegetables in basements, cellars, outbuildings and pits. The various facilities are discussed and maintenance methods suggested. Temperature, moisture control and handling are outlined; in addition, the booklet provides storing tips for specific fruits and vegetables.

Ask for: "Storing Vegetables and Fruits"
Send: $1.00
To: Consumer Information Ctr.
Dept. 135J
Pueblo, CO 81009

Kitchen Tools

A 64-page catalog for people fascinated by kitchen tools. The catalog lists many kitchen utensils and some garden tools – items such as canners, convection ovens, food-drying racks, fluted vegetable cutters, pasta makers and planter flats. Ordering information and forms are included.

Ask for: "The Garden Way Country Kitchen Catalog"
Send: 25¢
To: Garden Way Catalog
Dept. A115F
Charlotte, VT 05445

BEST BETS
- Kitchen Carousel – holds 40 kitchen tools and knives; spins around
- Apple parers and nut crackers
- Canning tools
- Scales
- Sausage-making kits & equipment
- Beer-making equipment
- Stacking freezer baskets

Indoor Gardening

Cacti

A 38-page catalog of cacti and succulent plants with a free packet of cactus seeds. Hundreds of nursery plants are listed alphabetically by Latin name, with descriptions and over 300 black-and-white photographs. Some books, publications and supplies are also listed. Complete ordering instructions and order form are included.

Ask for: "K & L Cactus Nursery Mail-Order Catalog" **and** sample packet of seeds
Send: $1.00
To: Cacti & Succulent Catalog Offer
K & L Cactus Nursery
12712 Stockton Blvd.
Galt, CA 95632

Cacti & Succulents

A 48-page catalog of cacti and succulents. An enormous variety (over 1000) of plants and seed mixtures are carefully described; black-and-white photographs add to the charm of this catalog. Cactus and succulent collections are also available, and an order form is included.

Ask for: "Henrietta's Nursery Catalog"
Send: $1.00
To: Henrietta's Nursery
1345 N. Brawley
Fresno, CA 93711

Epiphyllums

An unusual catalog listing over 300 types of Epiphyllum hybrids. The catalog includes detailed tips on growing and rooting these plants, which are similar to but need distinctly different care than the desert cacti. Also included is a list of their flowers. The hoya and the rhipsalis are also available through this catalog.

Ask for: "Beahm Epiphyllum Gardens Catalog"
Send: 50¢
To: Beahm Epiphyllum Gardens
Dept. FS
2686 Paloma St.
Pasadena, CA 91107

Violets

A 22-page catalog focusing on African violets. More than 50 varieties of violets are available for purchase. The catalog also includes all the information necessary for successful care of these plants. A list of growers' supplies and books of interest is also provided.

Ask for: "African Violets & Grower Supplies"
Send: 50¢
To: J.R. Anderson
The Green House
9515 Flower St.
Bellflower, CA 90706

African Violets

A 15-page catalog of African violets, including variegated, miniature and trailer varieties. The catalog has full-color photographs of the blooms, along with descriptions and prices. It also offers accessories, culture information, books and an application form for the African Violet Society of America. Order form and information included.

Ask for: "Tinari Greenhouses Color Catalog"
Send: 25¢
To: Tinari Greenhouses
2325 Valley Rd., Box 190
Huntingdon Valley, PA 19006

BEST BETS
- Amigo: A brilliant red maroon single star, with bronze tailored foliage.
- Dazzler: A bright, intense, fiery pink with sugar white edge. Heavy double-flowering, sturdy foliage. Excellent show-type cultivator.

Terrarium Plants

A 4-page catalog of carnivorous and woodland terrarium plants. A variety of woodland terrarium-plant kits and carnivorous terrarium-plant sets are available, as well as certain rare plants, seeds and related items.

Ask for: "Carnivorous and Woodland Terrarium Plants"
Send: a 9" self-addressed, stamped envelope
To: Peter Pauls Nurseries
Canandaigua, NY 14424

Indoor Gardening

Carnivorous Plants

A 12-page, illustrated catalog of carnivorous (insect-eating) plants, ranging from the relatively common to the exotic. The catalog provides tips on successful culture of the various species offered. Also available are supplies and accessories for growing carnivorous plants, as well as books on the subject.

Ask for: catalog
Send: $1.00 (refunded with order)
To: Carnivorous Gardens
Dept. MP-81
P.O. Box 331
Hamilton, NY 13346

Unusual Plants

An informative, 22-page catalog and culture guide to rare and unusual houseplants. Each plant is carefully described, and color illustrations enhance the catalog. General suggestions about light, humidity, temperature, watering, soil, feeding and fluorescent light are included. An order form with instructions is also provided.

Ask for: "Kartuz Greenhouses Catalog"
Send: a postcard
To: Kartuz Greenhouses, Inc.
1408 Sunset Dr.
Vista, CA 92083

Exotics

An 8-page catalog of exotic seeds and plants. Included in the listings are instructions for the most successful growing of each seed. Mercury vapor lights are also available as an accessory to aid your seed-growing.

Ask for: catalog
Send: a 9″ self-addressed, stamped envelope
To: The Banana Tree
715 Northampton St.
Easton, PA 18042

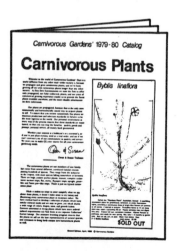

Carnivorous Gardens' 1979-80 Catalog

Carnivorous Plants

Byblis linaflora

SOLD OUT

GROWING MIX
This is the soil-less mix we use for all our plants: 2 quarts sphagnum peat moss, 1 quart vermiculite (horticulture grade), 1 quart medium or coarse perlite, 2 T. ground limestone. Remove the lumps and twigs from the peat moss. Thoroughly mix the ingredients and store the mix dry until used. Moisten the mix with a weak fertilizer solution just prior to use.

BEST BETS
- Bananas
- Palms
- Kaffir plums
- Brazilian peppers
- Macadamia nuts
- Chinese vegetables

Rare Seeds

A fascinating, 30-page catalog for plant lovers interested in growing exotics from seeds. The catalog lists nearly 150 plants, everything from the giant snake lily to the sausage tree. It provides instructions for 7 methods for sprouting seeds and hints on the causes of germination failure and seedling loss.

Ask for: "Rare Seeds Catalog"
Send: $1.00 (refunded with order)
To: John Brudy's Exotics
    P.O. Box 1348
    Cocoa Beach, FL 32931

Houseplants

A foldout that tells you how to select the right houseplant for the area you will be placing it in. Charts in the foldout show which plants grow best in different environments according to the humidity, temperature and light. The foldout also lists plants that can withstand abuse and those that do well in various special environments.

Ask for: "Houseplants, An Environmental View"
Send: a 9″ self-addressed, stamped envelope
To: Information Div.
    West Virginia Dept. of Agriculture
    Charleston, WV 25305

ENVIRONMENT
Pick a room in your house – the kitchen. Now consider the environment. Humidity is high from steam produced by cooking and dishwashing. Usually light is medium to dim because kitchens often have curtains blocking out the light. So find a plant that prefers medium or dim light and high humidity.

Houseplants

An illustrated, 8-page tabloid on the "Care and Selection of Houseplants." Basic facts about indoor plants as well as specific information on light (natural and artificial), temperature, water, humidity, soil, containers, feeding, repotting, trouble shooting, acclimation, diseases and insects are provided.

Ask for: "Care and Selection of Houseplants" (Pub. 1012)
Send: a postcard
To: Ms. Nancy B. Sweet, Pub. Editor
    P.O. Box 5404MSU
    Mississippi Coop. Extension Service
    Mississippi State, MS 39762

HOW TO WATER
The most convenient and efficient method of watering is to pour water on the soil surface and allow water to move evenly through the soil structure. Water from the household or commercial tap is suitable in most instances for interior plants. However, never use cold water. For best results, use lukewarm water which is near room temperature.

Indoor Gardening

Indoor Gardening

A 48-page booklet on indoor gardening. The topics include detailed descriptions of indoor gardens, including their location, stocking and care. Photographs and illustrations enhance the booklet, and a comprehensive chart describing decorative plants for the indoor garden is provided.

Ask for: "Indoor Gardening" (G220)
Send: a postcard
To: Publications Div.
Office of Governmental and
Public Affairs
U.S. Dept. of Agriculture
Washington, DC 20250

Indoor Lighting

A 17-page booklet on indoor gardening using artificial light. The booklet tells how to create an environment with the proper temperature, humidity, ventilation and light and lists houseplants that do best under artificial lights. Also includes a section on starting vegetable seeds indoors.

Ask for: "The Inside Story on Growing Plants"
Send: 25¢
To: Duro-Lite Lamps, Inc.
Dept. FS
17-10 Willow St.
Fair Lawn, NJ 07410

LIGHT

The combined light and dark period each day (called photoperiod) has a major effect on plant maturity. Some plants prefer long days and short nights; others, the reverse; whereas some like equal day-and-night periods. So, choose plants needing similar amounts of indoor sunshine. Many common houseplants will grow and flower on a 12-16 hour light period.

Indoor Lighting

A 12-page booklet on indoor gardening using a Gro-Cart with a fluorescent lamp. The use of electric light in plant growth is discussed, and examples of plants which have been successfully grown under fluorescent lamps are included. A list of Gro-Cart models, fluorescent fixtures, accessories and miscellaneous items is provided.

Ask for: "Gro-Cart Indoor Lighted Garden Cart"
Send: 50¢
To: J.R. Anderson
The Green House
9515 Flower St.
Bellflower, CA 90706

Growing Violets

A foldout telling how to grow African violets. Includes the suggested light for an abundant bloom, proper watering, necessary humidity, soil, air and temperature. How to propagate and culture African violets is also explained, and the various diseases and pests are listed.

Ask for: "How to Grow African Violets"
Send: a 9" self-addressed, stamped envelope
To: Buell's Greenhouses, Inc.
P.O. Box 218MP
Weeks Rd.
Eastford, CT 06242

TEMPERATURE

Temperature is ideal at 65° to 70° at night with a 5-10° rise during the day. Temperatures below 60° for any extended period will slow the growth. If too high, plants will grow sappy and spindly with too few blooms, which drop before gaining good size. Better a bit cool than too hot, expecially if humidity is low.

African Violets

Catalogs and information about African violets. Gives recommendations about light, water, temperature, humidity, fertilizer, soil mixes, pots, grooming, varietal selection, insects, diseases and companion plants related to African violet culture. Scores of varieties are offered for sale, accompanied by beautiful photography. Plant supplies also available.

Ask for: "Tips on Growing African Violets" **and** catalogs
Send: 50¢ (in stamps or coin)
To: Fischer Greenhouses
Oak Ave.
Linwood, NJ 08221

FLUORESCENT LIGHT

Fluorescent light works well with violets and related plants. Cool and warm white tubes, 8-10" above the plants, work best. Lights should be on for 12-14 hours daily. A general rule is to provide about 15 watts of fluorescent light for each square foot of growing area.

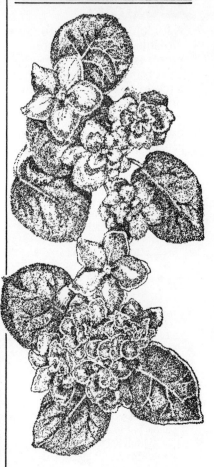

Indoor Gardening

Gloxinias

A foldout telling how to grow gloxinias. How to pot the plants is thoroughly explained, as is the general care of them, such as the proper light, the proper watering and different cycles of growth that can be expected. Seed and vegetative propagation are also explained at length.

Ask for: "How to Grow Gloxinias"
Send: a 9″ self-addressed, stamped envelope
To: Buell's Greenhouses, Inc.
P.O. Box 218MP
Weeks Rd.
Eastford, CT 06242

WATERING
When soil is dry to the touch, water thoroughly until the water runs out the bottom of the pot; do not water again until soil is again dry to touch. Use lukewarm water. Do not allow pot to stand in water. Spray foliage with lukewarm water to keep it clean; sun on wet leaves will cause spotting.

Oleanders

A brochure on oleanders and the Oleander Society, plus an information sheet on propagating oleanders. The illustrated information sheet provides a detailed description of the oleander and various methods for its propagation. The brochure contains some additional tips, as well as details about joining the Oleander Society.

Ask for: "Know Your Oleanders" brochure and "Oleander Information Sheet"
Send: a 9″ self-addressed, stamped envelope
To: National Oleander Society
Dept. MP
P.O. Box 3431
Galveston, TX 77552

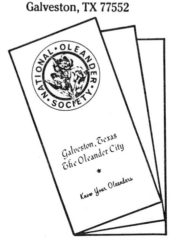

Orchids

A brief illustrated foldout that explains how to identify the major families of orchid plants. The material also gives tips on growing. An application for membership in the American Orchid Society is enclosed. Membership benefits include the society's monthly magazine, advice from experts and an 80-page book on orchid culture.

Ask for: "Your Guide to Orchids"
Send: a 9″ self-addressed, stamped envelope
To: American Orchid Society
Dept. FSFG
84 Sherman St.
Cambridge, MA 02140

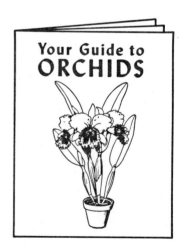

Poisonous Plants

A 10-page booklet that explains how plant poisons affect people, what to do if poisoning occurs and how to avoid being poisoned. It provides a chart that describes the poisonous parts, the toxic principle and various symptoms of poisoning for many common plants, flowers and trees.

Ask for: "Plants with Poisonous Properties"
Send: 50¢
To: U-35
College of Agriculture and
Natural Resources
Storrs, CT 06268

Fuchsias

An information sheet on the culture of fuchsias and a sample copy of *The Fuchsia Fan,* a monthly publication of the National Fuchsia Society. General information and helpful hints for cultivation are provided in the information sheet.

Ask for: "The Culture of Fuchsias for Fun and Beauty" and *The Fuchsia Fan*
Send: a 9″ self-addressed, stamped envelope
To: National Fuchsia Society
Dept. M
3774 Vineyard Ave.
Oxnard, CA 93030

NEW PLANTS
Young fuchsia plants need only to be tip pinched, not pruned the first year. They should be staked when needed, or trained for the form wanted. Do not fertilize newly planted fuchsias until they have started to grow in their new location; 2 weeks following planting is suggested.

Reprinted with permission of the National Fuchsia Society.

Plants News

A sample issue of the colorful monthly magazine, *House Plants & Porch Gardens.* The magazine includes a question-and-answer column, book column tips, projects, classified ads and glossary, in addition to feature articles on such topics as plant movement, Boston ferns and Crassulas. Contains lots of color photographs.

Ask for: a sample copy of *House Plants & Porch Gardens*
Send: $1.00
To: House Plants
P.O. Box 428F
New Canaan, CT 06840

BUG JUICE
Puréed bugs make a remarkably effective pesticide. Collect as many plant pests as possible (a quarter-cup of mealybugs will take you quite a while). Throw the insects into a blender with a cup of water. Mix, chop and purée. Spray the mixture on infested plants. Organic gardeners say that this "bug juice" works wonders.

Indoor Gardening

Greenhouses

A 28-page catalog displaying "lean-to" and freestanding greenhouses, as well as accessories for heating, cooling, ventilation and insulation. The greenhouses may be enlarged or reduced in size. Also listed are such accessories as thermometers, benches, sinks and timers.

Ask for: "Greenhouse Catalog"
Send: a postcard
To: Aluminum Greenhouses, Inc.
Dept. FS
14605 Lorain Ave.
Cleveland, OH 44111

Greenhouses

A 24-page, full-color catalog of redwood/fiberglass greenhouses, accessories and supplies. Both attached and freestanding greenhouses in a variety of styles and shapes are available, as are supplies including heaters, exhaust fans, books and plant stands. A 20-page booklet on selecting a greenhouse is also included.

Ask for: "Greenhouseman Catalog"
Send: $1.00
To: Peter Reimuller — The
Greenhouseman
Dept. FS
P.O. Box 2666
1900 Commercial Way
Santa Cruz, CA 95065

LOCATION
Generally the greenhouse should be positioned so that it receives the maximum amount of winter sunshine. However, the shade cast by nearby buildings and trees and the difference in the angle of the sun's rays in summer and winter must be considered.

Solar Panels

A catalog for solar-panel greenhouses that can also be used for heating. The catalog explains how double-panel, acrylic/fiberglass panels make this greenhouse so efficient. The catalog offers both freestanding and lean-to models, as well as accessories. An abundance of color photographs and letters from customers are included.

Ask for: "It Runs on the Sun — And Not Much Else"
Send: $1.00
To: Vegetable Factory
Dept. FS
P.O. Box 2235
New York, NY 10017

Solar

A color handout and a 15-page catalog for greenhouses made of a double layer of acrylic. They explain the advantages of this design, offer letters from satisfied customers and present several different greenhouse models. The catalog also contains a chart to help determine how much it will cost to heat your greenhouse.

Ask for: "Catalog and Color Brochure on Sunglo Solar Greenhouses"
Send: a postcard
To: Sunglo Solar Greenhouses
Dept. F-1
4441 26th Ave. W
Seattle, WA 98199

Soil Nutrition

An informative, 18-page booklet about the nutrition of greenhouse crops. The booklet covers soil testing, limestone and soil pH, the pH preferences of greenhouse crops, composting, fertilizer mixing, systems for continuous fertilization through watering, preparing fertilizer stock solutions, deficiency symptoms of some plant nutrients, and more.

Ask for: "Nutrition of Greenhouse Crops"
Send: 75¢
To: U-35
College of Agriculture and
Natural Resources
Storrs, CT 06268

Greenhouses

A 13-page catalog with a 4-page price list describing hydro-garden greenhouses and greenhouse equipment. In addition to listing prices and specifications of equipment, the catalog explains a soil-less system for growing plants and the design of an energy-efficient greenhouse.

Ask for: "Home Greenhouse Catalog"
Send: a postcard
To: Hydro-Gardens
Dept. G
P.O. Box 9707R
Colorado Springs, CO 80932

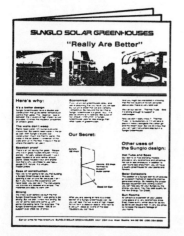

FERTILIZER

Fertilizer is inexpensive. Less than 3% of the cost of producing a greenhouse crop is spent on fertilizer and application. Since fertilization costs so little in the production of a high-quality crop, ideal nutritional levels should be the goal of every grower.

Indoor Gardening

Hydroponics

A packet of information on hydroponic gardening—that is, the growing of plants without the use of soil. Explains the advantages of this type of gardening and how it works. Also included is a catalog that lists hydroponic products and greenhouses, plus a booklist.

Ask for: "Hydroponic Information"
Send: a 9″ self-addressed, stamped envelope
To: Aquaponics
Dept. S
28119 Dorothy Dr.
Agoura, CA 91301

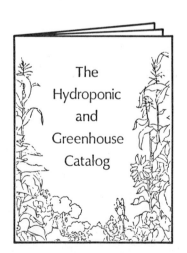

The
Hydroponic
and
Greenhouse
Catalog

Hydroculture

An assortment of packets dealing with various forms of hydroculture. Some of the material is concerned with commercial hydroponic growing systems, while other information covers hydroponic grass and sprout systems. One packet is directed at those interested in home hydroponic systems, and a fourth packet offers information on supplies and components.

Ask for: "Hydroculture Packet"
Send: $1.00
To: Ronald E. Chalfont
Hydroculture, Inc.
P.O. Box 1655
Glendale, AZ 85311

ADVANTAGES
Among the advantages of hydroponic growing are the superior taste, quality, appearance and extended holding quality of vegetables, made possible by giving the plants optimum feeding and environmental conditions. It is also possible to grow anything that grows in soil year round!

Hydroponic Kit

A kit that includes everything that you need to grow a hydroponic tomato plant. The kit includes seeds, a starting pot, a 6-month supply of agricultural nutrients and a set of simplified instructions. This kit will give you first-hand knowledge of how hydroponic gardening works.

Ask for: "Hydroponic Tomato Kit"
Send: $1.00
To: Aquaponics
Dept. S
28119 Dorothy Dr.
Agoura, CA 91301

Index

Index

Use This Form to Get Your "Free Stuff"

Here's a form that will make it easy for you to send away for some of the items in this book. Make photocopies of this page, and use the bottom part each time you send in a request that's accompanied by either a long, self-addressed, stamped envelope or money (or both).

Date _____

Dear Sir/Ms.:
Please send me the following item, which was listed in Free Stuff for Home & Garden:

_____

_____

I have enclosed (check which and fill in amount):

☐ a long, self-addressed, stamped envelope

☐ _____ for postage and handling.

Name _____
                                          (please print)

Street _____

City _____ State _____ Zip _____

FREE STUFF BOOKS

FREE STUFF FOR KIDS
Over 250 of the best free and up-to-a-dollar things kids can get by mail:
- coins & stamps
- bumper stickers & decals
- posters & maps

$3.45 ppd.

FREE STUFF FOR COOKS
Over 250 of the best free and up-to-a-dollar booklets and samples cooks can get by mail:
- cookbooks & recipe cards
- money-saving shopping guides
- seeds & spices

$3.45 ppd.

FREE STUFF FOR PARENTS
Over 250 of the best free and up-to-a-dollar booklets and samples parents can get by mail:
- sample teethers
- booklets on pregnancy & childbirth
- sample newsletters

$3.45 ppd.

FREE STUFF FOR HOME & GARDEN
Over 350 of the best free and up-to-a-dollar booklets and samples homeowners and gardeners can get by mail:
- booklets on home improvement & energy
- plans for do-it-yourself projects
- sample seeds

$3.45 ppd.

FREE STUFF FOR TRAVELERS
Over 1000 of the best free and up-to-a-dollar publications and products travelers can get by mail:
- guidebooks to cities, states & foreign countries
- pamphlets on attractions, festivals & parks
- posters, calendars & maps

$3.45 ppd.

Craig Olson's
DECORATING WITH PLANTS
Creative, simple ideas for decorating with plants and caring for them—from the most entertaining plant expert in America. Illustrated and indexed.

$3.45 ppd.

Books By Vicki Lansky

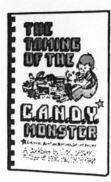

Hundreds of parent-tested ideas for the first five years. Includes topics such as baby care, feeding, self esteem and more.
Spiral bound. $4.45 ppd.

The most popular baby book and tot food cookbook for new parents. Includes over 200 recipes and ideas.
Spiral bound. $4.45 ppd.

The classic cookbook that helps you get your children to eat less sugary, salty junk food...and like it!
Spiral bound. $4.45 ppd.

The most complete, up-to-date, helpful, entertaining and gifty baby name book ever. Includes over 10,000 names. Introduction by Erma Bombeck.
$3.45 ppd.